SMALL ROOMS AND OTHERS

Essays by J. Bryan McGeever

SMALL ROOMS AND OTHERS

Essays by J. Bryan McGeever

Contents

"God put me in a position to make a fool of myself, but no one expected me to take such glorious advantage of it."

Dalton Trumbo

One Last Tour[i]

My family's house was almost empty. The rest, items my parents could live without, would be sold today piece by piece. They needed the cash to help pay for the move. It was a tag-sale inside our home, strangers shuffling through rooms, eyeballing furniture and bric-a-brac. Then, by the end of the day, it would be one more suburban tract house owned by the bank. My mother couldn't bear it, so I came to pick her up. My father would remain to manage the sale before shutting the door for good.

I parked on the street in front of the mailbox and waited, wanting no part of this surreal event. Should I wander inside a house full of bargains hunters, my gut instinct would be to start tossing bodies like a crazed bouncer. With no means to bail my parents out of this mess, I gripped the steering wheel and stared straight ahead.

To see my mother's face was to view my own 19 years later: the cut of her jaw, the bridge of her nose, the same blue eyes. I was her only child and knew exactly why she was taking so long. She was saying goodbye to the place, visiting rooms she'd carefully decorated, bidding adieu to birds and squirrels she'd fed each day in the backyard. Hers was a wildly beautiful creativity that had become unhinged through drugs and depression. I was hoping for a quick getaway, but instead I waited. There was still time for one last tour.

That cherry tree in the middle of the yard was a housewarming gift from my great-grandmother. Just beyond its branches was the window to my room, where I dreamed awfully big, suffered my first hangover, and lost my virginity. The hallway light was usually on while I slept as a kid. Mom would come home late from her waitress shift, doggie bag in one hand, wad of cash in the other, holding it up to the light.

"Remember those cleats we put on layaway? We can pick them up tomorrow."

The den where the family dog died in my arms was at the opposite end of the house. Adjacent to that was the kitchen, with an old rotary phone that once shook the foundation: Dad, I got jumped tonight driving the cab. Can you get out here?" A part-time college job that had gone horribly wrong. I still don't know how he did it, pounding the ambulance doors and screaming my name before it pulled away.

Then, years later, by that worn-out patch of grass, Dad and I fought like demons, an unnatural act that will haunt the rest of my life. I don't know the exact moment when my parents became partners in drug abuse. It may have developed over time, or perhaps it was always there, carefully hidden away from me. After that fight, the two of them shut the door, pulled down the shades, and quit everything.

Cocaine has a way of possessing human souls, inhabiting them completely before pummeling them into the ground. My mother was incoherent. My father was plain evil. I stayed away for two and a half years. The only news I received was when bills arrived in the mail for credit cards I didn't have.

It was the house that offered the slimmest bit of hope. One Christmas I buzzed through the neighborhood to check for signs of life, a single string of lights blinking back at me like a vessel trapped in sea smoke. They twinkled in my rearview as I sped up the block, the quickest holiday get-together ever.

When I was younger and still capable of hero worship, I'd track down the haunts of great authors, their houses, pubs, and hotels. I'd stand on sidewalks or sit in my car for minutes at a time and wait for the magic to start. Now? How 'bout now? It took me years to come to my senses, realizing I was just staring at husks and fragments of other people's lives.

Even today I persisted in old habits. The classroom where I taught in Brooklyn this past year had the Empire State Building framed in one of its windows. I ate lunch each day atop my desk, taking in its majesty and waiting for Kong to appear. In the afternoon, I'd drive past the house where "Sophie's

Choice" was filmed, never glimpsing Meryl Streep in any of its windows. It was just a pretty house in a quiet neighborhood.

So the thought of knocking on a stranger's door someday, asking permission to view my own snakeskin, left me distressed. I'd made the mistake of doing my student-teaching at my former high school, pondering old lockers and gazing out at the football field. In time it became nothing more than the building where I was learning to teach. I didn't want that to happen to our house. The moment my mother got inside the car, we'd pull away for good.

When a relative called after nearly three years to tell me my parents were sober and making a comeback, I didn't know how to receive it. There'd been other comebacks in the past. I made tentative arrangements to visit my mother at the facility where she was being treated for depression. She'd been undergoing electroconvulsive therapy, an intense treatment that could leave her suffering from amnesia. I knew very little about it other than the horrific "Cuckoo's Nest" images I conjured in my head. The three of us sat in the visiting room like strangers and chatted politely. My mother looked tired and haunted.

Her roommate had been sneaking boyfriends in at night, and my father was trying to have the room switched. I remembered how gently he tended to her and how much older they looked.

I started to visit regularly. The therapy seemed to be working, and my mother eventually went home. We slowly morphed back into a family, even poking a bit of fun at ourselves. "Hey, remember that time on the front lawn? Good times, boy…" They met my fiancée and came to love her. She couldn't believe these were the same people I'd stayed away from for so long.

Life was returning to normal except for that one constant of nearly 40 years. My father had refinanced the house prior to their troubles. The money had been spent, and the new mortgage exploded. They were in their 60s, healthy and sober, with two weeks to vacate the premises.

My mother finally emerged from the house, my father in tow carrying her things. I could see strangers behind them in the doorway darting back and forth as more cars pulled up to the curb. I took her bag and nodded toward the house. "Have they picked us clean yet?"

My father grinned at my melodrama, as though the house wasn't filled with jackals and grave robbers haggling over silverware. "It's just crap," he said, "a bunch of stuff we don't need. We're movin' on, pal. This is a good thing."

With the three of us outside and the house crawling with strangers, the place was already taking on a foreign look. My mother and I headed for the car. Across the street was a neighbor's house that had been filled with girls when I was a kid. They'd occasionally invite my younger, lunatic self over for a movie. Opposite their television was a window, framing our house in the same way I'd one day view the Empire State Building.

I had always wondered what they thought of the small family across the street. Over a period of decades, they'd seen me flip over handlebars, jump off rooftops, and blow up mailboxes with fireworks. They'd had ringside seats to a front-yard brawl and seen ambulances light up the sky for one mishap or another.

Shouldn't we be leaving something behind, something other than buried pets and a collapsed swimming pool? Maybe a plaque of some kind: *The embattled McGeevers slept here from '73 to 2011. The parents had their demons. Their kid was wild with delusions of grandeur. But they loved each other hard, survived every misadventure, and then simply drove away.*

J. Bryan McGeever

I've slain dragons. But when we arrive to the theater freshly scrubbed, we can't help breaking another rule by smuggling in a third. My new family fits comfortably inside two seats, our baby's first show, and one more New York trifecta.

Any Kid in the City[iii]

The students enter the building through a side door, submitting their backpacks and any personal items to the NYPD safety-agent who receives them at the steps. There's a male agent for the boys, a female for the girls. Everyone is scanned for weapons, cell phones, and drugs upon entering the building. Some of the more committed students have hidden items inside a shoe, their underwear, maybe the lining of a wig. The rest have scattered belongings in various spots throughout the neighborhood. It's Monday morning at one of New York City's Level Five suspension sites. I teach English here.

I used to comment to friends that I'd gladly teach any kid in the city. When I made this remark, I was working at a large, traditional high school in New York. We had sports teams and a band. We sang carols to the kids before the holidays. I signed yearbooks and hugged parents at graduation. Then mayoral control hit our building like a maelstrom. The school was declared dangerous and inefficient. The faculty was forced to transfer and find new positions. So how do I describe this strange, new teaching universe I've entered, one that was not my first choice? It's become the greatest lesson on human dignity I've ever had.

My current school has a unique and troubled population, but they still have a right to an education. They earn credits at this suspension site. They take their state exams here. We study the motivations of Holden Caulfield, the original troubled New York teen, like we would at any other school.

Yet the drama unfolding in their neighborhoods often takes precedent over any literature in class. If a student loses a friend to violence, he might wear a t-shirt with the departed's face staring back at me, rendering the book in my hand useless. If I offer someone a pen with blue ink, he might decline because it's not his neighborhood's colors. Symbols are everywhere, and home is all that matters. They resent being here and pine for their regular schools all year long. They argue over things I don't understand. They make comments in the middle of a lesson that shake me to the core. So as the student body files into the building kid by kid, and the scanner hums and beeps over every pocket and curve, I must find a way to chip away at mistrust, anger, and hostility.

At sixteen, I went to work washing dishes in a Long Island restaurant where my mother waited tables. The owner was also the county's district attorney, a man who ruled his business much like a courtroom. During an impromptu kitchen tour, I was observed wearing cut-off jeans and reprimanded. Tired and sweaty, I answered back and lost my first job. As the owner marched me through the kitchen and out the back door, he made a remark that stayed with me forever. "You just wait...We'll see what becomes of you!"

Years later, during my student-teaching experience, I encountered my first unruly kid. He showed up late, talked incessantly, and pushed his assignments to the floor. Still a student myself, I was dumbfounded. As I bent to retrieve his work, it struck me how easy it was to slip into the district attorney's role from my dish washing days, to turn my back, and root for this kid's downfall.

That summer I pulled into a 7'11 and there he was, half asleep against a wall, a can of malt liquor the size of a baby's arm beside him. He was wasted and bleary eyed, but still managed to recognize me and say hello. I recalled my earlier prediction and how I couldn't wait for it to come true. I returned to my car to watch him nod off again, the cheapest victory ever.

So perhaps I could be more flexible in the classroom. It's time to recognize that intelligence assumes many forms. Not everyone has to love Salinger. Holden's language is getting a bit dated and Jay-Z probably now lives in the Caulfield's apartment overlooking the Park. And when a boy in class obsesses over his time spent at Riker's Island, sometimes the best response is to lay down the book and listen.

"Mista, in the showers…everyone wears boxers. And if the soap drops, you jus' say, 'Fuck it,' and leave it there."

<u>Important Facts to Remember:</u>
1. There is always plenty of soap at Riker's Island.
2. The section reserved for minors segregates according to race and gang affiliation.
3. If another boy wants to fight, you cannot ask the C.O. for protection because he's already securing a room for the brawl to take place.
4. Should you ever back down from a fight, be prepared to be called a punk for the rest of your life.
5. If you hope to last as a teacher in a level five suspension site, the lesson of the day does not always come from you.

Americans have always enjoyed a good comeback. Even New York City's Department of Education believes in redemption, allowing students to apply for early dismissal from suspension if they qualify. Like anything worthwhile, it comes with rules. The students must apologize for what they did in an essay. It's not surprising that every kid I've worked with is completely innocent of all charges.

"Mista, I didn't do it. It wasn't me. That other kid is lyin'...and my school jus' don't like me."

"Would you like to get out of here early?"

"Yeah."

"Then you need to make your peace with what happened, redo this second paragraph, and apologize with feeling."

By the end of the week, C. approaches to say goodbye. Today is his last day. He's served his suspension and will return to his home-school next week. His regular building is five stories high with a river view of the Manhattan skyline. Our site is two hallways with eight kids per class. In twenty-four hours, the boy's world will expand tenfold. He makes his way through the building, a hitch in his step, shaking hands and saying goodbye. Whenever a student prepares to leave, we invariably tell him the same thing: "Congratulations...and don't come back."

As C. takes his final strut, I can feel the entire hallway holding its breath, rooting for him. The mission statement here is no different than any school in the country, the rewards just the same. As time passes, as it does for us all, we'll eventually see what becomes of him.

J. Bryan McGeever

The Lords of No Discipline[iv]

We are a small but hearty bunch of New York City teachers. Our classrooms are tucked inside the crevasses of the largest education system in the country, in old Department of Education office buildings and school basements. It takes a certain kind of teacher to work at the DOE's Alternate Learning Center. Most people call our sites "suspension schools."

Nowadays my ALC colleagues and I often face empty classrooms- and it's not because the city's toughest students are behaving better. It's because Mayor de Blasio and Schools Chancellor Richard Carranza have resolved to keep disciplinary suspensions to a minimum, claiming that ALCs are a way station on the school-to-prison pipeline.

Suspensions are down fifty percent. Students committing outrageous misconduct often stay in their regular classrooms. Remember when cursing out a teacher was a very big deal? Well, now it's just Tuesday.

But what if ALCs aren't a wasteland of unwanted children on the path to ruination. What if the city's suspension centers are actually productive places dedicated to smashing the school-to-prison pipeline? What if City Hall's virtue-signaling policies are based on myths?

25

The first myth is that suspended kids don't get an education. The notion of permanent expulsion-tossing a kid away until some noble educator or politician rescues them- is the stuff of Hollywood teacher movies. Nor do suspension centers offer the urban equivalent of "Lord of the Flies." There are no fight clubs at the ALC or steel-cage matches. No one is releasing children into the wild to decide the swiftest and the strongest.

Here's how it actually works. When children are suspended, instead of reporting to their home schools, they show up at an ALC- where they'll find an entire school community waiting for them.

Guidance counselors and social workers. Five major subjects, as well as online classes. We use restorative talk circles to help break the cycle of poor decision making and have visiting speakers who grew up in the same neighborhoods as them. We take field trips to view parts of the city they normally wouldn't see. They can even call our school aide "Mom" if they wish. Many do.

All these children have to do is take different buses to different schools until their suspensions are complete. On their final day, students write an essay about their time with us and what they've learned from the experience. The stigma created by the mayor that school suspensions are the beginning of the end for a child is simply part of the man's continuous melodrama.

Then there's the matter of systemic discrimination. If a student believes they've been targeted for suspension due to race, religion, or ethnicity, the student should be aware that their school doesn't have that kind of power. An independent hearing officer assigned by the DOE listens to both sides and determines whether a student gets suspended and, if so, for how long. The school can make a recommendation for suspension, but ultimately the officer decides the penalty. If a student is still not satisfied, they can apply for a transfer.

During my fifteen years as a teacher in New York, my supervisors have been mainly women of color- strong, competent, highly educated products of city schools themselves. Women who are married to black men. Women who are raising black boys. Does the mayor really believe these women would tolerate students of color being targeted for suspension? Is he suggesting they're major players in some grand racist conspiracy?

Does he think these women wouldn't be the first to speak out if Hizzoner's theory were true?

The last myth is that schools with high suspension rates must be out of control. Again, not true. A high rate simply means that problems with certain students are being addressed by an ALC.

A superintendent suspension does not have to be a stepping stone into the prison system. I wouldn't work at an ALC if it was, and neither would any of my colleagues. A fifty percent drop in school suspensions is an excellent talking point for a politician seeking a national platform but does little for the school system that needs him back home. A mayor who refuses to discipline students properly because he may face political scrutiny is an abomination.

J. Bryan McGeever

The Brownie Caper^v

I once took the New York City police exam on a whim. In the suburbs of Long Island where I grew up, a large portion of high school buddies already had badges and guns by their early twenties. "Dude," an acquaintance would say at a local tavern, "I shot my gun off the Brooklyn Bridge at three in the morning...It was awesome!" I'd played football with this guy in high school. He used to shoplift wearing his game jersey and last name stitched on the back.

Although from the perspective of a substitute teacher earning fifty bucks a day, his boast was intriguing. The undeniable fact that I would never possess a cop soul meant nothing to me at the time. I had no desire to fire rounds off iconic bridges at sunrise, but the allure of Gotham and a steady paycheck were prime motivators. I signed up for the test.

Over a year went by before I was to report to the academy, an antiquated, converted public school in Gramercy Park. Only my interest had waned by this time. The vetting process was lengthy, my background investigator intrusive, and I'd just received a fellowship to a fine writing program. I belonged somewhere now, and it wasn't sitting

29

before a detective explaining the origins of a fight I'd had in the eleventh grade.

Yet I still continued to show every time an official letter arrived, the interviews and finger prints, the psych evaluation and eventually the fitness portion at the academy. My outsider status was apparent the moment I arrived. In a meadow of frozen brush-cuts, my hair flopped down to the jaw. When it was time to fire a dummy pistol at a dummy assailant, I was the only lefty. An instructor asked me if I had at least sixty college credits, I declared three times that amount with the pride of an English school boy.

Irony took its stance once the mile began. The track was small and narrow, eight laps instead of four. The first leg was slow, so I took a commanding lead; a pleasant runner's high settling my nerves. Here was where I might finally have a say: The best guy for the job was the one no longer interested.

I started to lap the pack, those lumbering stragglers in back, and then everyone else. Then I lapped them again, thoroughly enjoying myself by now. By the final sprint, I was determined to crush the others into a fine blue paste beneath my track shoes. I caught my breath, picked up my stuff, and left, relishing the moment when I would tell them no thanks. Until the phone rang one fateful day.

"Sir, this is *Detective Hassle*[1] from the NYPD. It seems there's a last-minute concern with your employment record."

"Sorry?"

"Apparently you ate a brownie without asking."

"A what?"

"A fudge brownie, sir, from your previous employer...You were terminated but never mentioned it in your paperwork."

"I didn't think it was relevant."

"Well, the restaurant did. According to them you were fired for stealing."

"But...it was a brownie."

"Nevertheless..."

The unauthorized brownie, I remember it well. It was covered in whipped cream and sprinkled with walnuts. It was made of luscious chocolate fudge, and it went down smooth.

Allow me to explain. I needed a second job to supplement the teaching. Raised on a waitress' tips, I've always held restaurant work in high regard. It turned out, however, that my mother's skills were not hereditary. I turned out to be the worst server in the history of food. On the night I was preparing to quit, I'd been eyeing that brownie for hours. There were rules, of course, one cheeseburger allowed per

---

[1] Detective Hassle appears in this essay under a pseudonym.

shift. But I'd never eaten any of mine. I figured twenty-five burgers were the equivalent to at least one brownie. Not so. I was fired that evening, a scandal apparently that I would never live down.

I suppose it was kind of a relief. At long last my fugitive days were over. The NYPD had cracked the case wide open. My character was called into question, and I was declared unfit for the academy. All that time I thought I was in the lead, it was actually me who was being lapped, sunk deep in a chocolaty mire of my own doing.

In later years I've taught numerous composition classes to college students who needed their final credits for the police academy. In the margins of their papers where I made my comments, I invariably felt obligated to warn them of the perils of illicit baked goods. Shoot as many rounds off the Brooklyn Bridge as you like, just be mindful of temptation, those pies cooling in a perp's window, the fresh doughnut in a child's hand. Look away, Recruit, look away...

All That They Can Be?^{vi}

The local recruiter is at my classroom door, and I wish he'd stop doing this. When I explain that there are designated areas throughout the building for him to speak with students or 'potential recruits', he apologizes profusely. In fact, his etiquette is always spit-shined and gleaming, like something he's learned from a book or heard at a seminar. He shows me his visitor's pass, carefully smoothed against a lapel, and apologizes once more. Never again, he says. It's just that this time it's important. Could he please have a word with Ernesto?

I'd like to believe I have the final say on these matters, but Ernesto is already out of his seat and calling the man sir. His normal slouch has been corrected, and a hand keeps his jeans from dropping below the waist. They shake hands, and a heartbreaking glow washes over the kid's face. I quietly shut the door while they confer in the hallway.

The pride of belonging to a military family is important to me, yet I still see these recruiters as something of a threat to public schools. A salesman in a crisp uniform is still a salesman with a quota, be it used cars or young, beating hearts.

I know this man is just doing his job and that Ernesto is looking out for himself. If he does sign up, he'll have housing and benefits. He'll experience teamwork and the art of discipline, something he's sorely in need of learning. I also know that Ernesto's father is not in his life, and that his recruiter is probably aware of this. His mother works tirelessly to support him. Perhaps business at the local recruiter would not be quite as good if his situation were different. Suddenly there's this man, this confident guy in a uniform who knows where he stands in an uncertain world, and he's waiting in the lobby, the hallway, the school library, because he explicitly wants to know how *you're* doing and what *your* plans are for the future.

In 2015, the Army recruited 1,440 high school graduates into active duty from NYC, Westchester County, and Long Island. I realize that federal law and city regulations require that military recruiters get the same kind of access to students as trade school and college recruiters. What bothers me is the recruiter's sense of unregulated access. In fact, in 2007, school officials reminded principals that military recruiters should not be "given unfettered access to students in classrooms, cafeterias, gyms, or other areas of the school building," according to The New York Times.

Of course, some students will enlist. Most often, it's the quiet ones who return to show off their uniform, clean shaven cheeks and bristly heads peeking into a doorway. The faculty always stops to make a big deal: *Hey! They're he is! Do you have any idea how proud we are?*

When Ernesto's time comes, he can't wait. He's finally outta here! But did his recruiter somehow best me? Did I fail the boy by not steering him in another direction? I think about it every time it happens, fifteen years and counting.

"Look, Ernie, take care of yourself. Make sure you visit after boot camp."

And then...

"Hey...don't go looking for trouble, okay? No Superman stuff."

He gives me a smile and one last fist bump. Then it's down the steps and out the door.

Ernesto appears in this essay under a pseudonym.

Small Rooms [vii]

There's plenty of porn here, stacked neatly beside a DVD player, polished, spray-tanned bodies that fail to arouse. Opposite the flat screen TV is a small couch, a loveseat really, but I prefer to stand. The entire space is laughably small, more janitor's closet than state of the art fertility clinic in Manhattan. "Down the hall and to the left," said the technician. "Press the buzzer when you're ready."

Just like that, a carefree adolescent discovery is transformed into the single most important event of my life. It doesn't make you go blind after all. Sometimes it can shape your destiny. Decades ago I would have led a childless existence. Now, through in vitro fertilization, I have a chance to negotiate with nature, to perform inside this booth slightly larger than a confessional, and then suffer its consequences or celebrate its joy. Like any underdog faced with overwhelming odds, I'm feeling a bit woozy.

I reach inside my satchel for my own stash, DVDs purchased for this special occasion, a vintage classic from the seventies, shapely platinum-blondes seducing handymen and astonished pizza boys, and a Brady Bunch parody for some levity, where Alice-the-Maid turns out to be quite a vixen.

The plastic cup for my sample isn't much bigger than a shot glass, and it's within reach on the counter. Lurid images flash on screen, accompanied by a groovy, percussive soundtrack. There is enough lube here to slather my entire body, slip through a crack in the door, and make my escape if necessary.

Everything is where it should be, everything is just right—except for my head. I consider the technician down the hall. I don't want to keep him waiting. I ponder the receptionist scheduling new clients and the sobs of the heartbroken whose efforts here were futile, one woman crying for her mother when she received the news. I obsess over the drugs inside of me, something called Clomid to stimulate sperm production, and I curse the Cialis that's currently losing the fight. I recall the blunt conversation my fiancé had with her mother when we discovered our little problem. "See," she said, "I knew it wasn't you."

Scene after scene unfolds, and all I do is stare down at myself and tremble. Truth be told, I'm completely dumbfounded, consumed with the knowledge that I *am* the one to blame for this. This isn't the first small room that's changed the course of my life. At seventeen, the only thing I wanted to be was big. My first Google search for male infertility and anabolic steroids produced this headline: *Public Enemy #1*, an endeavor so fruitless it can be used as a contraceptive. So, I'm poised half-naked and sweating, flaccid and filled with dread, while an endless loop of porn plays before me, the perfect punishment for my vain and hollow selfishness.

***

I used to tell myself that I was an athlete, not a jock. I didn't stalk the hallways of my school wearing my game jersey. I didn't push smaller kids into lockers for fun. I trained alone, long and hard, like it was religion. Somewhere along the way my obsession ran too deep. I stumbled down a wormhole, entering the realm of the Long Island muscle-head.

The guy who ran our gym was huge, and back then huge was all that mattered. He kept a picture of himself in his barren shoebox of an office that my friends and I would gaze upon. There he was, number Ninety-Seven, posing with his teammates, the 1987 scab replacement team for the New England Patriots. It didn't matter that he'd played during an NFL walkout and that fans had jeered when he took the field. We didn't care that he'd never recorded a single tackle in NFL history, or that he referred to women as "pigs" and wore his sweatpants up to his ribcage to conceal a layer of fat. None of this mattered to the kids who were in awe of him. He was Ninety-Seven on that wall and number one in our hearts.

Since I was always there, I took a job cleaning up, vacuuming, straightening dumbbells, and polishing the machines. I'd work out for a while, then go paint a wall. Do some push-ups, sweep a hallway. On the night of my senior prom, instead of renting a bad tux and getting drunk with friends, I did backflips on a trampoline until it was time to lock up and go home.

Ninety-Seven's presence was everywhere, his top-heavy, pigeon-toed frame cruising the aisles, barking insults to teenagers who took it as high praise. After hours, a tribe of men would convene outside his small office, bouncers, bodybuilders, and semi-pro has-beens, all of them sporting the same brutish beefiness as Ninety-Seven. They'd comment on each other's physiques until the door opened and everyone got what they wanted. One evening I was invited inside. I understand that it was done simply to keep me quiet, but at the time I considered it an honor. I came to be known as *The Experiment*, and I cherished this nickname as though it actually meant something.

Every subculture has its time worn traditions. Ninety-Seven dispensed drugs the way the Godfather granted favors, humbled men standing reverently before his desk while he filled a hypodermic needle with synthetic testosterone. He'd inspect each syringe for bubbles then beckon the next in line to step forward. Each stunning, narcissistic moron would then offer the Head Moron a slab of rump to inject. "Bryan," he said to me that night, "if you ever tell anyone about this, I'll put your head through that wall."

The hormone that had been inserted into me was a man-made, oil-based solution administered by a 23-gauge needle. Anabolic steroids interfere with male fertility by tricking the body into thinking it doesn't have to produce its own testosterone. The follicle stimulating the hormone is never released, and the body produces little to no sperm. These effects are reversible, but only if one is mature and wise enough to stop taking the drug.

That summer I reported to college training camp with the same enhanced muscles you might find on a racehorse. I'd taken shots to get big and pills to get *ripped*. When it was time to bench press for the weight coach, I did as many reps as any linebacker, hefting weight that my tendons and ligaments were never designed to support. There was no reason for a punter/placekicker to be that strong. I'd become a tightly wound, juiced-up fraud. Years later, football long behind me and Ninety-Seven's gym closed, I continued to take an over the counter steroid called androstenedione. It wasn't as potent as the injections, but it kept my delusions of male strength and virility alive. In fact, the only reason I stopped was because it was made illegal.

***

I'm standing here up to my neck in irony and it serves me right. This wasn't a single mistake I can attribute to youth. I've earned this defeat over a period of decades. In desperation, I switch DVDs and try again. It seems impossible that anything good will come of this.

The premise of the next movie is ridiculous and for some outlandish reason exactly what I need, fake college pledges riding clown-like bicycles down a hallway in the nude, ponytails swaying, naked knees pumping high. Lo and behold, a stomach clenching specimen is produced and secured inside the container. I ponder the scene once more before turning it off. The extraordinary effort these women put forth into balancing atop those bicycles will never be forgotten. I truly hope every one of them has moved on to brighter things.

I discover later that what little sperm I produced had very low motility. It wouldn't swim and had to be injected directly into my partner's eggs, resulting in eight B+ fertilizations and one precious A. The technician appears and I make the handoff.

And what of the woman who will have these eggs placed inside her uterus anticipating a healthy pregnancy, the one who administered fertility shots to her abdomen for twenty-one days, suffering headaches, blurred vision, and nausea only because I was unable to resist the temptation of small rooms, the one who found the clinic, made the appointments, and never judged or questioned her partner's foolish past? She prefers to stay out of it. It is the one and only condition to her unconditional love. Should anyone ask for her version of this narrative, she would not have one. She did what needed to be done and that is all.

Before exiting the room, I decide to pay it forward, leaving the DVD inside the machine for the next anxious hopeful. My fiancé and I have run the gauntlet. After insemination, all of New York City becomes our waiting-room.

***

In the great expanding mansion of my life there is a hallway containing three small rooms. The First and Second are forever sealed and the only one that matters is the Third. Our one and only perfect *A* now stands for Aubrey. Her room is warm and cozy and guarded by *Mickey*, the wilds of Brooklyn just outside her window. She's already a smart and fanciful girl about town, a being so lovely her sleeping form puts me in awe, slumbering peacefully in a world that's already hers.

A Happy Death[viii]

I'm dying up here. My first crossover from writer to performer, and I'm about to go down hard. Beside me stands a Viking named Valdor wearing a horned helmet, t-shirt, and jeans. Valdor stalks the boards between sketches, adlibbing one-liners in a valiant attempt to protect us from comedy's archenemy, but *silence* is everywhere. While he wins a sympathy chuckle from someone's mother or best friend, pity has a short life span. It's colder up here than I imagined yet I cannot stop sweating. The Viking retreats off-stage, and my sketch begins. With one blow from the kindly brute's sword, he could put an end to all this suffering. Instead, he lets the audience take care of that.

After completing a sketch writing class at the People's Improv Theatre, I signed up for Battle Sketch, a competition featuring sketches written and performed by the scribes themselves. The winner is determined by an audience vote, returning the following month to "defend the crown."

The sketch I entered was odd and puerile. A hapless schlub named Mr. Deepwell has his prostate examined, yet no one can find it, doctors, nurses, John Travolta, etc. After four pages of hijinks, a mythological creature named Sketchopotamus appears and hunts down the elusive treasure.

In the green room before the show, performers hastened to fill their cast list, asking fellow competitors if they'd play a role or two.

"Hi... Would you mind playing a monster called Sketchopotamus?"

"Sure."

"Do you think you could play him in a distinctive bass-baritone, the bastard love child of Barry White and Frankenstein's monster, with a touch of Bowzer from Sha Na Na?"

"I guess."

This would not be the startling debut of a bright new force in American comedy.

And really, I should have known. Funny how the mind works, blotting out lost battles for decades, sleeper cells of shame waiting to be called into action at the weakest points in our lives. As I prepared to go on, it occurred to me that I had been here before. I had a flashback to my freshman year at Stony Brook University. I was a young idiot who barely spoke a word, a member of the football team, and magnificently immature. So I took a drama class. Unlike others who'd wandered on stage to realize their calling, energized by the applause and the camaraderie of belonging to a troupe, I remained a young idiot determined to prove his idiocy to anyone who may have doubted it.

I auditioned for a part in *The Madwoman of Chaillot*. I wore the costume they gave me, barked out a few lines, and pursued every female member of the cast. I had real arguments on stage, made faces at teammates in the audience, and tilted my fedora back so it wouldn't mess my hair for the after-party. I was an abomination.

Since then I've tried to make amends, developing into an avid theatregoer and the drama gods were appeased with one stipulation: *Come as often as you like but step one foot on stage, anywhere on the planet, and we shall cast our vengeance upon you.* I honored this agreement for years, appreciating the masters and behaving like a gentleman. Years went by and I thought I could get away with it. The PIT theater is small and subterranean, with more performers than audience members. Who would know?

But the gods were slumming that night, and the jig is quickly up. My actors flub and misfire their lines. There are awkward pauses and lifeless utterances. The flow is off, the timing non-existent, and my beloved Sketchopotamus is more Cookie Monster than primordial beast with a thirst for human glands. I can't understand it. My three-year old thought this sketch was hilarious.

I'm also there solo. I have no one in the audience to ham it up for me, no one to pat my back and tell me lies. I have no acting training to speak of, beyond that episode of *Friends* in which Gary Oldman teaches Joey the finer points of dialogue: "When you enunciate, you spit! That's what real actors do!" My one saving grace is not to fight it. I will die a happy death and wipe the stage clean.

I've cast myself as Deepwell, a role I was born to play. As each actor has a go at me, I slobber and shout with unwarranted gusto. When Sketchopotamos appears to save the day, I let out an operatic cry of joy until my body goes limp. A silence unbeknownst to man rises from the audience and infuses the stage, a nothingness so profound no one, not even Shakespeare or the Greeks, could withstand it. And yet I count the evening a success. Not only have I paid my debt to the gods, I've reaffirmed my rightful place in the theatre world: the audience.

JAMES GANG[ix]

The last time I saw James up close he was punching me in the face repeatedly. My rationale for such a resounding loss was that James was older, one of those fabled 'left-back' kids that sprang from the halls of Norwood Elementary like weeds of iron. James taught me a valuable lesson about violence, one I instill in my own students in South Jamaica, Queens: *The tougher you think you are, the further you are from the truth.* Sometimes they listen. Sometimes they have to meet their own *James.*

So when I came upon an article about his death, I felt the sting of his punches all over again. It was written four years ago by some tough guy columnist in a New York paper. His claim was that living on Long Island was a myth, our neighborhoods and schools, even our beaches. Somehow James was the embodiment of this myth, the monster we had created and deserved. Juicy tabloid stuff, but James would have found trouble in Hampton Bays or Wichita, Kansas. He was that kind of kid.

We sat alphabetically in class. A pair of Jameses with similar surnames, we became fast friends. Our tract-housing development was fairly new, so we'd play war after school in the surrounding woods and sandpits. We were both fair-haired and easy to confuse. Sometimes he received my grades at school.

Other times I got blamed for beating up some kid when it had been his handiwork. As we grew older and became strangers, I occasionally wondered what my doppelganger was up to. It turned out James had been incarcerated for twenty years prior to his death.

The last time I saw him alive was from a distance. He was hanging upside down from a streetlamp in a strip-mall parking lot, challenging the world to a brawl. We didn't say hello. A few years later he would be convicted for four robberies, specializing in stealing cash and drugs from pharmacies. Four years ago, he announced a holdup at a Seaford pharmacy, brandishing a pellet gun that looked like a 45. He was shot by an off-duty cop, which also resulted in the friendly-fire death of a federal agent. I'm sure the store he was robbing was occupied by women and children. The columnist described James as a "bag of human garbage."

Fair enough.

But the strange thing about garbage, especially when it comes from one's own backyard, is that it's difficult to throw away. The thing's broken, holds no value whatsoever, but hangs around for some reason, in a shed, an attic, or the back of someone's mind. James and I were two of the most disruptive boys in the history of our school, but there was something different about us. At eleven years old, it was just a hunch that my spare time would best be spent away from James. The last time we played

together was at his house, two years before our
Three O'clock High bout. The hours wore on and I
abruptly made my way for the door. "Hey," he said,
"aren't ya stayin' for dinner?"

"No, thanks, Jimmy. I gotta get goin'."

Book Review: *The Noble Hustle: Poker, Beef Jerky and Death* by Colson Whitehead[x]

Those who read Colson Whitehead's new memoir, *The Noble Hustle: Poker, Beef Jerky and Death,* searching for the latest how-to book on Texas hold 'em or a straightforward account of The World Series of Poker are in for a surprise. It isn't written by the latest guru or moonlighting celebrity. The author will not be cluing us in on stratagem or mind-blowing philosophies. This is a tale told by an outsider, a creature of metaphor and simile set upon a unique subculture. He'll report to the mother ship in his own distinct tongue and we are welcome to observe. This is indeed a memoir about the World Series of Poker, yet be forewarned: any college dropout who heads to Vegas with this book in tow will find himself trapped inside a vortex of his own doing.

With a suicidal monarch on the cover and a bone chilling first line, Whitehead's journey begins. "I have a good poker face," he says, "because I am half dead inside." This is a statement we might expect from a no-name gunslinger riding into town or perhaps something less than human. Zombies are big now. So is poker. Whitehead offers both.

In an essay for The New Yorker in 2012, Whitehead makes an assertion regarding his life's work that lends a great deal of insight to this book. "An artist is a monster that thinks it is human," he states. We learn that as a child, the bestselling author of *Zone One* preferred to stay at home absorbing an array of bad cinema until he came upon a genre called *Psychotronic,* a hurried, low budget style of horror-science fiction that mesmerized him. "They were unaware of their utter freakishness," he explains, "unaware that the world found them absurd...If these movies existed, then surely whatever measly story was bubbling in my brain was not so preposterous."

This breakthrough offered the young writer total freedom to develop a style of unique observation and lightning quick prose packed with boundless pop culture references. When admitting a desire to establish a "King Kong" persona at the poker table, he confesses, "On the Simian Scale, I was more Bubbles the chimp, break-dancing for cigarette and gin money before Michael Jackson rescued him from the streets." The author is just getting started, fine tuning an engine of revved up witticisms and one-liners.

Whitehead freely admits to being no poker expert. He is a better than average player who enjoys a friendly game with writer friends. When a magazine editor offers to bankroll him the ten-thousand-dollar entry fee for the World Series of poker, he accepts. There will be no other payment for his account of the experience.

He decides upon Atlantic City, "Vegas' little cousin," as an excellent training ground for the big competition and goes searching for his people, the monsters and unrepentant losers that inspire him, before he even arrives. Unfortunately, New York's Port Authority has cleaned up a bit, offering little to none of its former infamy. "I could be anywhere," he laments, "starting a journey to anyplace, a new life or a funeral." He climbs aboard a state-of-the-art *Greyhound* and ponders his chances as "one of the most unqualified players in the history of the Big Game."

Whitehead's mind really starts to twitch once he arrives at the *Tropicana Casino and Resort*. "The contemporary casino is more than a gambling destination; it's a multifarious pleasure enclosure intended to satisfy every member of the family unit." Despite intense makeovers to the culture and atmosphere of legalized gambling, Whitehead knows that diehards never change. "I found my degradation," he marvels. "I was among gamblers."

Here is where we find the author's monsters, something akin to Kerouac's "mad ones." They're the ones who've stopped pretending, a people of oblivious purity. They live life as they see fit, so incredibly un-cool that it somehow makes them wondrous. Whitehead approaches the table and sums up the competition as though he was describing a legion of superheroes: "Big Mitch is a potbellied endomorph in fabric softened khaki shorts and polo shirt…" "Methy Mike, a harrowed man who had been tested in untold skirmishes, of which the poker table was only one…" "And then there was Robotron, wedged in there, lean and wiry, a young man with sunglasses and earbuds, his hoodie cinched tight around his face…"

He joins them representing his own tribe; a dystopia he inhabits called Anhedonia (The inability to experience pleasure). "We Anhedonians have adapted to long periods without good news…We have no national bird. All the birds are dead."

By the time he's ready for The World Series of Poker in Las Vegas, Whitehead's hired a personal coach to administer crash courses, pep talks, and numerous conference texts. The man is taking this seriously and becomes enthralled with the unlikely desert oasis. "I recognized myself here. Monster places for monster people."

Due to his unique powers of observation and assessment, the reader considers the possibilities should Whitehead step away from the table to wander the cartoonish landscape. What would he think of tourists clutching two-liter margaritas, or of men snapping escort cards on every corner? With this writer the possibilities are limitless. But this is a memoir about Poker.

The author eventually learns staying power at the table, a core value he compares to writing. "In novel writing, biding is everything…Waiting years for a scofflaw eleven-word sentence to shape up into an upstanding ten-word sentence: this is the essence of *Patience*."

In time we discover the role that beef jerky plays in all this, and the influence corporate sponsors have on Whitehead's adventure. His odyssey concludes with an ending that film buffs may recognize from past decades. "But you know how '70s sports movies end."

J. Bryan McGeever

The Hidden Deal: Underground Poker on Long Island[xi]

The story was supposed to begin here at an illegal poker hall in Farmingville called *The River*, but *The River* ran dry and I was left staring at a blackened door with a mailbox next to it that said, FISH. It must have been a marker or tag for players to locate the building. Fish swim in the river, right? More than likely, *The River* was flowing somewhere else, but I had no idea where to find it.

"Everybody loves to gamble," said Peter Dunn, retired NYPD lieutenant. According to Dunn, the level of interest an illegal gambling activity generated from the law was based upon its organization. "We weren't concerned with the office Super Bowl pool or the neighbors playing a few hands," he said, recalling his years working vice in Manhattan South. "Our primary concern was any organized game where the house took a percentage. Some guys, if they're smart, can get away with it for a while. But sooner or later, everybody gets popped."

My contact at the casino wasn't old enough to buy beer, yet he'd been navigating the choppy waters of *The River* for over a year. He wore an ace of spades charm around his neck and had been counting the days until his twenty-first birthday since he was sixteen. "I can't wait to get to Vegas," he said, toting the latest poker bible around, quoting random passages. "It's a game of skill," he insisted. "I could make a living off this if I didn't have to go to school."

'Ace' just completed finals at an area college and was willing to take me to see a tournament. He said they'd have a few games running at once and that there'd be no problem getting in. A guy named Pretzels ran the house at *The River* and worked the door. Pretzels was a problem solver, and I couldn't wait to meet him. I was on my way when I got the call. "No good," said Ace. The casino was dark and no one was returning calls. "They must have been shut down. Sorry." He said he'd try to find another game, but I never heard back from him.

The River had it all, and I wanted it back. I needed to see how a tournament was run. I wanted Pretzels to size me up. All I had now was an idea.

I envisioned Long Island with an enormous deck of cards flexing above it, waiting to spring across two counties. It didn't take long before I found the right website. Suffolk County popped up within the New York listings, and I was on my way. Many of the locations described their atmosphere as 'friendly', which I assumed meant I could play without ending up in the trunk of someone's car.

I made several picks based on proximity and desired buy-in range ($300-$500), steered clear of the contact who called himself 'Goodfella', then admitted total beginner status to everyone. I had half a dozen offers by the end of the day.

***

The clock on the wall says eight-thirty, but the time here is always *now*. I'm somewhere in the heart of Suffolk County, Long Island seated at a poker table in some dude's basement. I'm taking in my surroundings and waiting for the goose bumps to settle. The Internet may have changed the world, but it'll always be a bit suspect. One minute you're on your way to play poker with strangers, the next you're changed to the wall of your new master's dungeon. The inside is decorated like any other basement on Long Island, a pool table opposite the bar, with support pillars, and cheap wood paneling. Pictures of Elvis, Marilyn, and James Dean swoon back at me. I could have gotten drunk here in high school. It's unclear at this point whether to be relieved or disappointed.

"Relax," says the guy in charge. "We play a friendly game here."

The dealer is a big guy in his forties who we'll call Mike. This is Mike's basement, and everyone here is his guest. He runs the game from his wheelchair and pays himself five percent of every hand. His guests can play until their money runs dry, drink as much beer and coffee as they like, while Mike's wife serves them lasagna warmed over a Sterno flame.

I pay my buy-in, handing over grocery, gas, and rent money. Anything is possible now. There are seven other guys at the table thinking the same thing, only they're totally serious about their chances. The conversation revolves around the evening's possibilities, all possibilities of the past, and any in the near future. There are tales of going bust in Atlantic City, beatings taken at Foxwoods, and last-minute winnings in Las Vegas. Someone mentions the chance of a casino being built on the Island's East End by the Shinnecock Nation and the room falls silent with possibility.

"Hey, you gettin' a job for the summer or what?" a heavyset lifer asks the baby-faced twenty-something to my right.

"Me? A job? Why would I do that when I can be checkin' and raisin' all summer long?" Laughter spreads across the table like a free round of chips, the type of guffaws shared by men with similar addictions. A cell phone goes off three heads to my right. A tanned guy in his thirties answers, tucking his chin into the phone.

"Yeah," he says. "You knew this is where I'd be...I told ya I was workin' tonight."

It's high time to admit that I've never played a hand of poker in my life. I came here looking for a tale to tell and have more interest in the players than the game. My subjects, however, are into winning money the way I'm into a good yarn. I'll get what I want eventually—and so will they.

There's one thing I did in preparation, though. I created a starter kit for myself. Since my knowledge of the game began at zero, I went with the obvious choices. I bought a copy of *Poker for Dummies*, rented *Rounders* with Matt Damon, and found a decent memoir on the underground game called *Poker Nation* by Andy Bellin. My kit was heavy on atmosphere, but details on actual play were still whizzing past me. Damon loses the girl, but comes to terms with what he is, a card fiend, and heads out West for The World Series of Poker. Bellin introduced me to the underground life and taught me some important jargon, and chapter one of *Poker for Dummies* is just plain hysterical: *"Poker has always been a microcosm of all we admire about American virtue...Call it the American Dream—the belief that hard work and virtue will triumph....It is an immigrant's song, a mantra of hope; it is an anthem for everyone."*

Back in Mike's basement, the first hand is about to begin. I'm peering around the room, taking in all these proud Americans and sons of immigrants, and

I realize the true hunger of the place. Mike shuffles the deck and lays down the button.

My first two cards come sliding at me. I have two pair of something or other, but I'm not sure where it falls in rank. There's a crumpled sheet of paper in my pocket listing the hands from lowest to highest, but I dare not peek. Mike sees me holding my cards like a Hollywood cowboy, realizing my ineptitude by the way I repeat the phrase, "Hit me," like Danny Devito's character in *Cuckoo's Nest*. He tacitly agrees to be my interpreter, letting me know when to check, raise, or fold. After every hand, he tells me whether I made the right choice. Through some fluke, I end up winning the first two hands and the razzing begins:

"What kinda beginner's luck is this?"

"He ain't no beginner. This guy knows what he's doin'."

"I think I seen him at Binion's last week (hardcore casino in Las Vegas)."

"He's probably some kinda mechanic (slang for cheat)."

"Or workin' undercover for the bunko squad!"

"What exactly do you do?"

I identify myself as an English teacher, and the table does its best to mind its grammar and syntax from then on. When one of the younger players, a kid who'd been shoveling pasta all night, declares with a full mouth, "Yo, these freakin' meatballs are retarded!" his buddy looks him over. "Is that supposed to mean good?" The kid nods, wiping his mouth. "Well, maybe you could speak English from now on, so the teacher doesn't have to shoot himself."

I'm learning the game, making fast money, and winning new friends. I breathe deep and start to relax, then proceed to lose three-hundred and fifty dollars in around seventy minutes. My chips vanish at an alarming rate, the other players' grow high, and Mike clinks another five percent for himself and the Mrs. after every round. I take my beating quietly, thank the table for an interesting evening, and leave Mike's place for good.

It wasn't anyone's fault, really. Even with Mike's guidance, I'd shown very little patience, staying in hands just for the excitement despite having junk cards. There's a cherished quote that veteran players like to repeat. It was said in the movies I'd watched and the books I'd read, and it goes something like this: *If you look around the table and can't figure out who the sucker is, then the sucker is you.* But what do you call someone who volunteers for the job? I'd kissed that money goodbye before I'd ever stepped through Mike's door, considering it story money. I would eventually be paid three hundred dollars for this story, but lost three hundred-fifty. It cost me just fifty dollars for an experience I'll never forget. Mike, for his part, turned out to be a very good host. He was good at his job and seemed genuinely pained after I'd been wiped out. I wonder if he or any of the others could possibly understand a guy who set himself up on purpose, someone who actually wanted to lose. I wonder if their psyches could entertain such a notion.

"Well," they might say, "every deck has its share of jokers...Alright, who's in?"

J. Bryan McGeever

Cold Spring^{xii}

Sometimes I think this Hamptons mansion will become my Long Island Alamo. There are 21 steps leading up to its front door, providing an excellent perch to view oncoming invaders. It's getting warmer outside, and they'll be returning, rumbling down Sunrise Highway, crossing the canal like a castle's moat, world beaters fighting for their right to *paaaarty!* It'll soon be time to fix bayonets, wave the white flag, or simply turn and run. Thoughts of spring and summer have never given me the chills before.

I rent a seasonal room in a large mansion in Southampton. It's relatively cheap, across the street from school, and a wonderful place to write. It's certainly not the worst place to end up, the bottom tail of a fish called home, a final stronghold before the exile. This island is wet all over, yet once in season, there's nowhere else but here. Folks say the sun shines on the East End just like it does in Paris; these same people also have a famous bridge to sell if you're interested. My rent quadruples the moment that French sun arrives. People have been coming by recently to have a look.

My grandfather and great-uncle escaped World War II with a couple of Purple Hearts between them. They started a furniture store in Babylon sixty

63

years ago. There was this new concept when they began, a kind of experiment. Returning soldiers could finally leave the city. Babies could boom on their own front lawns, and the price was right. My ancestors filled these houses one by one. My parents comprised the next wave, cruising up and down those neat, orderly rows of conformity, letting their hair grow long. I used to study my mother's yearbook as a child, the frozen hairdos and white lipstick, that one dropout who played piano and wrote songs better than anyone could have imagined. He lives out by me now.

When I'm not teaching, saving the world from fragments and run-on sentences, I deliver furniture at my family's store. The original building is still there, a stubborn patriarch poised along the Sunrise. My buddy Tom and I travel up and down this fish's spine, hefting items into houses we could never afford to buy or rent. Apparently, the same Paris sun driving me from the Hamptons stretches all the way into Manhattan. It's a privilege to live on Long Island now. So, what do you do when you can't hold out much longer?

Not long ago, back in Hamptonia, I experienced an epiphany of sorts: three Baldwin brothers at once! Alec was starring in a play in Sag Harbor. Billy and Stephen came out to see him. Their big brother was incredible that night. I spent a good portion of the play just watching them watch him. Afterward, I wanted nothing more than to be an honorary Baldwin, strong, talented, Long Island royalty. They had made the move from middle-class Massapequa to "Hollywood East" almost effortlessly. Baldwins don't get kicked off Long Island, that's for sure. The whole thing seemed wonderful and completely impossible as I drove back home to where my days now are numbered.

So it keeps getting warmer, and there's nothing I can do to stop it. The last time people came to look at the house, I paused like Gatsby at the top of the stairs while they had a look around. Some broken butterfly wings lay scattered at my feet, a spider with a voracious appetite in a corner above my head. I stooped down, pressing the wings in a palm while would-be club promoters and sellers of designer oxygen cruised the kitchen. I wondered if they knew what a place this was to finish the rough draft of a manuscript or read a good book. I wondered if they knew that none of this would last or that the sun was ours and no one else's.

Look! Here it comes now. Everybody rotate.

Adia's Note^{xiii}

A new school year is on its way, and I did not get any of the classes I requested. My classroom's been switched from the second floor to the basement, and my attendance list has another teacher's name on it. The historic, NYC high school where I've taught English for five years is in the process of closing, whittled down each semester until all that remains is its leftovers. I used to read the morning paper before class while the sun spread across my desk. Now I'm staring at a sewer grate just thankful for a job.

If the teacher I'm replacing goes into remission, I'll be excessed from the building. If he dies, I get to stay. This is the new normal. Students were informed the previous year that the building was persistently dangerous and failing, and a mass exodus ensued. The overflow of teachers was shunted from the building according to seniority, handed their walking papers by indifferent secretaries. The only reason I'm still here is because my colleague is dying.

If I position myself just right, I can glimpse a portion of sky in the window. I have yet to meet my new students and begin to daydream.

Adia had just become a U.S. citizen when we met. A tall girl, with high, elegant cheekbones, who

often wore scarves and headdresses from her native
Guinea. She was my student for three semesters
because English was not her first language. She'd
return after each state exam, nearly four hours of
translating sentences from English to French and
back again, vowing the next time would be different.
From a statistical point of view, Adia was a
detriment to the building, one more student failing
big tests, when in reality she was one of its jewels.

In a school comprised mostly of students from
the West Indies, her small country in Africa was
exotic to them. Good natured rivalries over island
nations and continents would sometimes get ugly.
Adia responded by offering DVDs from a budding
African film industry. "See," she carefully explained,
"we have buildings, too. We have roads and
hospitals…"

It was during her final semester that her
attendance became erratic. She'd be absent for
several days, reemerge, and then vanish again. One
day she approached me in the doorway, handing me
a crumpled memo, saying, "Please…you can never
tell anyone."

In a country where my morning paper continues
to shrink and the magazines I still read are
overflowing with glossy ads, the blunt force of a
single sentence on a wrinkled note hit me like a fist:
*The above patient was recently examined to monitor
the effects of genital mutilation.*

She was absent the next day and the one after that. It still shames me to admit how curious I was about the details: How old was she at the time? Who would allow such a thing to happen? I signed the note and handed it back. "Okay," I said, "I promise."

As I struggled to process what this young lady had shared, I realized the situation's enormity. Adia's class had recently finished reading *The Color Purple,* where a minor character suffers genital mutilation. Without knowing that one of my students had fallen victim to it, I'd offered my American male's perspective in class, condemning, and blathering on. I'd even posted an article about a play on the same topic, Lynn Nottage's Pulitzer Prize winning, *"Ruined."*

"Mister," she said when I approached her to apologize, "nothing can be done."

That spring someone donated a carton of books to my freshmen classes, a memoir written by the new president. I started passing out extras to random students. Each time I handed one off, the student beamed down at it, clutching it tight like a family heirloom. Word quickly spread, and I was stopped in stairways and flagged down in halls. There were knocks at my door from kids I didn't know. "Are you the teacher with the books?"

If I had to guess, I'd say about half read it. Most just wanted to see his picture on the back and carry him around in their backpacks. I bought more when I eventually ran out, saving one for the absent girl in the front row.

"Adia, is this something you might enjoy?"

"Oh, yes, Mister. Thank you!"

Several years later, after the school had been closed and reopened in the mayor's new business model, I ran into Adia on a busy sidewalk not far from the building. She was already a junior at an area college and studying Finance. We ran through the usual script of teacher and former student, the exchange of pleasantries between almost strangers. "You know," she said, "I read that book you gave me," and I was pleased. I told her how proud of her I was before we merged back into our respective currents.

The book didn't save her, of course, and neither did I. In fact, I probably did everything wrong when it came to Adia. Back then I saw myself as a writer who just needed a job. I liked books, and I liked kids, so I thought I'd do some teaching. I often stood at the head of class with nothing more than a case of jangled nerves and a patchwork plan. When it came to my student from Guinea, I was just an observer. She'd entered my classroom a somewhat damaged yet finely tuned instrument and left the same way.

***

My brand-new students are peeking into the room now, this afterthought of a classroom, pop-eyed freshmen looking down at their schedules and back at me. "Yes, I know, another teacher's name is on your programs. Relax. Everyone's in the right place."

Adia appears in this essay under a pseudonym.

J. Bryan McGeever

A Fan's Statistics[xiv]

Two times per year the New York State English Regents Exam visits the high schools of our fair city, four comprehensive essays over a period of two days, and this January's results are in. In my building, preparation for the exam begins in the ninth grade and continues right until the students enter class to take the exam.

"Hey, Mister—" a voice will call down the hallway just minutes before the test, "who wrote about those mice and men? George Steinbrenner, right?"

Due to the No Child Left Behind rule, everyone takes the exam during junior year, regardless of their proficiency in English. The student who's been in the system since kindergarten takes it, as well as the child who recently arrived in America whose second, third, or fourth language might be English. Whether they have designs on going to college after graduation or going on to become mechanics and electricians, they are going to sit for that exam.

The more students a school gets to pass, the better the school looks. As a result, many schools have pushed up the date for students to take the test. Rather than taking it for the first time in June, why not usher them in five months early and see what happens? If they pass, great, if not, get ready for round two. Better still, let's start grading the teachers on the results.

The Department of Education has been conducting a secret pilot program where twenty-five thousand teachers at one-hundred and forty city public schools are being measured without their knowledge on student performance on standardized tests. Sadly, the local media has weighed in with typical comments and clichés regarding the teaching profession. "Imagine teachers treated like other professionals—having their performance monitored and quantified," writes Adam Brodsky in an op/ed piece for the *Post*. In his late January article, Mr. Brodsky even cites Tom Brady of the New England Patriots as a good lesson to all of us regarding the power of impressive statistics. But the city recently discovered, in the most stunning way imaginable, that gaudy, blown-up stats aren't everything.

Despite his condescending attitude toward teachers, Brodsky still raises a good point. So, let's 'monitor 'and 'quantify' some of my students on their recent performance on the English Regents exam then determine my net worth once we're through. Out of five classes taught this past semester, I had one class of juniors, three groups of sophomores, and one senior elective. The juniors were an interesting bunch, bright, friendly, and respectful, one of the most enjoyable classes I've ever taught.

But before we can examine their performance on the test, as well as my accountability, we need to establish setting. My building was falsely labeled as an Impact School last year, which means it is now regarded as one of the most dangerous schools in the city. Coincidentally, before the DOE can get its hands on a building and chop it up into 'smaller learning communities,' it must first get it labeled as dangerous.

Once a school is branded as Impact, a script is then followed to shut the place down, and Phase I is complete. Security is intensified. Letters are sent home to parents, notifying them that their child may transfer out of a 'dangerous' building if he or she chooses, and incoming freshman opt to go elsewhere when it's time to select a school. The faculty is left to shrug and wonder where all these dangerous kids are hiding but come away with nothing. The school's hallways then begin to shrink, teachers are excessed, and the budget is cut. The atmosphere becomes bleak, like something out of an old Western. It's time to shoot the horses and circle the wagons because the enemy's closing in.

Yet the DOE machine keeps rolling. During Regents week, my school was notified that a 'new' school will exist inside of our eighty-year-old building next year (Phase II complete). It will be the same building, the same amount of kids, just with an imaginary border put into place, a brilliant new version of divide and conquer. One of my colleagues recently began her graduate school semester. When she introduced herself and her school, the DOE official moonlighting as an instructor explained that she was familiar with the building and that the school's fate had already been decided. "Jamaica High School is a warehouse," she said. She then advised the teacher to stop battling the DOE, to comply with the inevitable, or transfer out.

A warehouse. Any adult who's witnessed children passing through metal detectors each morning then frisked with scanning wands, not because they're dangerous, but for political reasons, knows what an absolutely disgraceful remark this is.

Let's return now to my classroom of juniors and Mr. Brodsky's pomposity: "...Why not make teachers prove their worth?" Very well, but shouldn't instructors be given an equal playing field before they're forced to compete? Do Stuyvesant High School, Brooklyn Tech, or Bronx Science, three of the finest specialized schools in the city, have Jamaica's problems to contend with? They have waiting lists to get in, while Jamaica struggles with a two-year-long DOE choke hold. Whose test scores do you think will be more impressive?

As I scan the list of results, I find that my class ran the gamut, lots of highs and lows. Some overslept and missed the exam, while others arrived early and pulled off stunning victories. Jamal[2] got his 97, but Forrest received a 51.

As much as I would like to take credit for Jamal's grade, the truth is that he's a self-starter who sits up front, takes notes, and never misses class. Forrest, however, disappeared into the West Indies around holiday time: "Going to my country, bye." He was gone for nearly six weeks, missing all his Regents preparation. I'm sure he was visiting family he hadn't seen in a while, but should his extended vacation have any bearing on my teaching career?

There's also no need to congratulate myself when Clarissa scores a high 86. She's quiet, attentive, and likes to read. I did my job each day and she did hers. Or Victor who managed to get himself suspended for three weeks then recorded a 47. All four of these kids were in the same class, and all four of them are responsible for their test scores. Not their teacher.

When it comes time to give Jamal's family a call to congratulate them on their son's success, I find out that he lives in a group home. I'm taken aback on the phone. I expected to speak to the man Jamal identified as his father on parent/teacher night, but he was just the counselor on duty.

There's no way to explain Jamal. He defies DOE logic and statistics. He left his group home

---

[2] All students appear in this essay under pseudonyms.

each morning, reported to his 'persistently dangerous high school,' where he was scanned, frisked and instructed to readjust his belt in the auditorium, then sat down to record one of the highest scores in the state. The kid's a winner, a true New York Giant, and I would love to bask in his glory or dance in his victory parade, but I'm nothing more than a fan.

J. Bryan McGeever

Taxi Wars^{xv}

I'd just finished changing my second flat tire, each spare as worn out as the first. The cab I was driving was a sickly lime-green and required no keys. At the start of each shift, I simply turned the ignition and took off. The car had neither heat nor air-conditioning, the day-driver leaving it on empty with a big, toothless grin. Everyone was addressed by a number. Mine was 19, which was also my age.

"Would you mine dropping me off at the corner?" said a young student as we turned onto her block. "My parents would kill me if they knew I used this company."

Understood.

As a student at Stony Brook University during the late eighties, I drove a cab part-time for the infamous Tootsie Taxi, operating from an ancient depot at the Stony Brook train station. The hours were flexible, the driving liberating, and best of all— no rules. Ask any lifetime resident of the Three Village area about the cabs that prowled the streets of Setauket and Old Field thirty years ago and their eyes might go wide. "Yes," they'd say with a shudder, "I remember Tootsie."

Oddly enough, the company had no competition, and 19th century historian, Lord Acton, must've had Tootsie in mind when he said,

77

"Absolute power corrupts absolutely." Customers were crammed into cabs like circus clowns, prices set on a whim, and one of the dispatchers, a man obsessed with the sitcom *Taxi*, refused to give us calls unless we called him *Louie*.

I was not immune to the company's mad ways, skidding into my share of garbage cans and mailboxes in the snow. I'd fall asleep in parking lots during the wee hours and Louie would send out a search party, a firing squad of headlights surrounding me until my door was yanked open. "Hey, 19, stay awake or go home!" To prove my worth, I'd drive down a flight of stairs on campus to make the next train. Ugly, mean, and dangerous, we were a company comprised of pirates and ne'er-do-wells.

One evening, a smartly dressed woman came off the train and entered the shack, the Tootsie nerve center, if you will. Louie and the boys were sipping coffee and watching porn. "My God!" she said. "This is supposed to be a business!" and headquarters exploded with guffaws. Tootsie was the only game in town. Until it wasn't.

When the competition arrived, the Stony Brook Rail became our Alamo. Their numbers were strong, their vehicles immaculate. They announced their presence by working the campus side of the train. In an unprecedented move that left us stunned, they drove customers home for free. Louie said they were run by the Mob. Louie, of course, was the first to jump ship.

As the competition lured drivers away, they were shunned. Unless we were tailgating and cutting them off. One evening, during the heat of battle, we were simply told to go home. The owner had sold them the company. The Battle for Three Village was over, and Tootsie's reign had ended.

But sometimes I stare at the spot where the shack once stood, listening to the cackles of a ghostly convoy barreling its way down Quaker Path, hunting down squirrels and hurling through stop signs, a toxic green mist of Stony Brook yesteryear.

Loaded Hallways[xvi]

The campus of my public school in New York City is a fortress these days. Gazing through the mesh caging of my classroom window, I spot faculty deans, campus security (a branch of the *NYPD*), as well as regular patrolmen walking the grounds like medieval sentries. As I move through the halls of this majestic, old building, I sidestep a trio of firefighters in full regalia, escorted through the building by two more cops, 9mm handguns bouncing off their hips. The students are unfazed, just life in the big city, New York's Finest, Bravest, and Brightest, all inside one building- but no one's sure why. Was there an incident today, a fire, perhaps, or robbery? That's really none of your business. Information will be doled out on a need to know basis, and welcome back to a brand-new school year.

Lunchtime. I enter the faculty men's room, a police officer's cap resting on a windowsill, its owner inside a stall, rapping to a prospective paramour. In the library, yet another officer. I grade papers. He argues with his girlfriend. I leave early to beat the rush, an officer sees me coming and turns away, referring to the wall as "sweetie," a high school suddenly transformed into the lawman's dating game.

It's not so much the constant cell phones, the squinting, suspicious looks as I enter a corridor, or the fact that no one notified the faculty of a police presence. It's those Glocks in their holsters, the 'hand cannons' at their hips. It looks obscene in our hallways. This place is supposed to be a sanctuary. Any drama coach will tell you, a few well-placed props changes an entire setting. I wouldn't dream of teaching *Macbeth* from the backseat of a squad car, so what are these people doing here with loaded guns? It's simply no way for a kid to go to school.

Last semester I had an opportunity to experience what the students go through. While snapping photos of the building for the school's literary magazine, I inadvertently stepped off campus. An *NYPD* van rolled up and demanded identification. I didn't have my wallet on me. Terms like 'pedophile' and 'terrorist' were used as casually as one might order a box of doughnuts. I countered with 'overkill' and 'police state' until my principal was called to identify me.

Yet this is the how many of our NYC's teens attend school. Instead of using the auditorium for assemblies and school plays, it's been turned into a waystation for students to adjust their backpacks and re-tie their shoes after running them through the metal detector. Maybe this indignity is worth the trouble at the airport on your way to vacation, but to Chemistry class? My first year in the building, the

AP of security proved how effective the scanners were by pressing one against the fillings in his teeth during a freshman assembly. Definitely a yearbook moment.

Once a building has been labeled an 'Impact School' the police arrive, and negative publicity ensues, which results in a failure to attract interested students. Low test scores soon follow, and another building is doomed. In order to avoid this vortex, many schools fail to report petty crimes inside their buildings. Ours was recently praised for its zero-tolerance policy on discipline. Everything from cell phone theft to verbal harassment was reported in good faith, and now the place is surrounded. Here at Jamaica High, *Catch 22* is not just a piece of literature.

The end of the day, my colleague and I start dishing on the day's events. Since the matter has never been addressed by administration, all we have is hearsay, whispered bull-sessions inside our classrooms. She tells me police guns were pulled on two students today. "'If I tell you to do something, you better do it,' was the matter of fact explanation. Then the officer asked her out to dinner.

All it takes is for one kid to have a bad morning, to carry that burden to school and act out on it, something that occurs throughout public schools nationwide. On most occasions this would lead to a routine suspension and call to home, with *NYPD* presence inside a school the end result could be a world of hurt that's become all too familiar.

On my way to the parking lot, I pass a flyer taped to the wall in an effort to win back the school, a graphic with a pair of hands gripping steel bars. *This is not a penitentiary*, it says. *We are students, not inmates...*

School Spirits^{xvii}

I've been teaching Writing and Literature in New York City's public schools for ten years. This spring, my former building will graduate its final class just shy of reaching the century mark. Thousands of students have passed through the building over the decades, many of their pictures still lining the school's hallways and trophy cases. It's impossible to conjure them all. So I'll focus on one.

Matthew was the star writer of the literary club, where I served as advisor. When he wasn't editing the school's newspaper or acting in a play, he'd submit essays equivalent to that of a seasoned adult. His writing was smooth and polished, possessing insight, integrity, and tremendous potential. Since many of the students attended the club for pizza and socializing, Matthew would stop by to drop off new stories and be on his way. He could have stayed to show off his superior skills, but he had no interest in that.

We began to edit his work privately, sometimes in person, often through the margins of essays handed back and forth in busy hallways. I wanted to show him the power of editing, rooting out those adjectives and adverbs that seduced many young writers. I told him about a professor I had in grad school, a brilliant essayist who could edit students'

84

work by simply closing his eyes and listening. I was delighted with Matthew's development and his efforts came to inspire me.

The years went by, and the boy only got better. We combed over advanced placement essays, college applications, and new material for the magazine. He took the English Regents exam as a junior and recorded one of the highest scores in the state.

By senior year, Matthew was so immersed in extracurricular activities that I saw him only in passing. One day, I handed him a flyer from one of the city's many teen writing contests. It was sponsored by a gay and lesbian organization that wanted themes specifically geared to their community. I presumed he would write something about marriage equality or gays in the military. He handed me his finished piece with the same matter-of-fact confidence as all the rest.

His story was about growing up in a strict, first generation family, and what it was like to openly discuss his sexuality with his father for the first time. He wrote about his initial trepidation, and the understanding and acceptance they eventually shared. Matthew had discovered his voice and was proud of it. He won the contest, then published it in a well-known anthology for teens.

We lost touch after that, although I drive by the school occasionally to admire its architecture and glimpse my old classroom. It's just a high school of the mind now, receding into memory as I head for my new building and fresh crop of kids. I still read Matthew's essay on occasion, recalling him and countless others, their spirits soaring well above the bell tower.

Jack Slept Here[xviii]

Let's you and I revolutionize American letters and
drink champagne with the Hollywood starlets...

—Jack Kerouac

If I listen to the trees sway outside his house, I
can conjure him up, speed-typing in his bedroom or
peering down at me from a window. Now that he's
gone, I can make him do whatever I want.

My car knows the journey by now, traveling the
North Shore route of 25A to Northport, Long
Island. A massive biography called *Memory Babe*
had directed me here originally. A picture of Jack on
its cover from when he was still handsome, before
his face bloated from booze and Benzedrine, his
good-looking mug in a perpetual state of brooding.
A lock of hair dangles down his forehead like some
doomed super-hero. Whenever I left the book on a
table, his eyes would follow me across the room.

I will always have unfinished business here in
Northport. This is one of the places where Kerouac
sought refuge after the big score. The backlash to
On the Road had broken his heart. "That's not
writing," joked Truman Capote, "It's typing."
Somehow in my delusions, I've made it personal to
me. Long Island lives in the shadow of NYC. We

have Seinfeld, Billy Joel, and a few Baldwin brothers. The fact that Jack slept here, a mere half-hour away from my hometown, will always thrill me. His pedestal period of fame was long gone by the time he'd arrived, eventually collapsing for good in Florida, "safe in heaven, dead." Northport reeks of his wine-soaked failures, but the years have a way of washing away defeat. His time in Northport is now considered folklore.

On my first visit, I'd shamelessly knocked on the door to inform the owner of the great author who'd once lived there. Fortunately, the man who'd purchased the home from Jack suffered fools gladly, allowing me to trudge across his property in the snow like a buffoon. There are two other former Kerouac residences in Northport, but they don't make the cut as far as ambience goes, modern vinyl siding and asphalt driveways. But this first one, with the high peaked roof and old wooden porch, is where I come to pay homage. It's been over fifty years since his voice reverberated throughout the house, over sixty since *On the Road* was published, a three-hundred-page love letter to America.

Sometimes, as I cruise the old block, I'll play one of his spoken word DVDs, his young man's voice filling up the car in an endless rush. You can actually hear him breathe during pauses, and I imagine the house sinking deeper into its foundation.

If one observes Northport at just the right angle,
it could pass for New England. Anywhere can look
like home if the proper spirits are consumed. Jack
would make the occasional romp to the ocean while
he was here, letting the girls on the beach know who
he was. But they never believed him. They wanted
'57 Jack, James Dean with a typewriter, not the
battered, middle-aged man who stood before them.
When his weekly allowance ran dry, he'd offer up
first editions of his books to the bartender at the
local tavern then pass out while conversation swirled
all around him. The bar hangs a poster of him now.

The inside of *Gunther's* on Main Street hasn't
changed much since his time here. Like most
workmen's locals on Long island, it's one long
rectangle. The bar itself is on the right, with tables
and chairs pressed along the opposite wall, and a
pool table in back. Decades ago, when Greenwich
Village had had enough of him, someone scrawled,
"Kerouac go home" on the bathroom wall of the
White Horse Tavern. Inside Gunther's, you may
still find "Kerouac come home" written by yours
truly several years ago. Jack looks tired and drunk
hanging up there on the wall, his head tilting back
to the right. There's a loftiness to his eyes despite
being half-closed, a man patiently waiting for "God
to show his face."

I've kept this laminated quote in my wallet for
years, something about revolutionizing American

letters and sipping champagne with starlets, something a young fool might keep until its edges have grown worn and yellowed. I press my face to Gunther's window to stare at him one last time. When I pull away, my breath leaves a circle of fog that evaporates in an instant. I walk down to the harbor, flinging the quote into Northport Bay like an old baseball card. Within a decade, Kerouac's home will grow a bit older, Gunther's will catch fire and burn to the ground, and I haven't been back since.

J. Bryan McGeever

Pretty as a Postcard^{xix}

When I open the windows to my classroom, the hum of traffic from the long Island Expressway fills up the room like rush hour forever. There's a postcard I've tacked to the wall beside the blackboard, an iconic photo taken by a man named Weegee. The picture teems with humanity, an entire stretch of beach filled with packed bodies. Row after row of people squint up at the camera and wave, Coney Island, circa 1938. Could I have had a relative somewhere in this immigrant stew, a friend of a friend of a friend?

My school's campus changes dramatically in the evening. I teach English to a boy from El Salvador during the day, his hard-working mother at night. Anyone with some energy left after a long day is welcome. This morning I counted shiny heads on a patch of grass during a fire drill. Now there are two men in white tunics outside my window facing east, a slash of Long Island sun dipping behind them.

Traffic continues to buzz as the men bow once more, the sky taking on the hue of a melted cream sickle. My students file into the room. No need to lament over the places I've never been for they're all right here, newly formed republics conferring with the smallest Latin American nations, Asia conversing with the Middle East. Continents shift before me as students takes their seats, smiling back like faces on a postcard.

Two night per week, I teach English as a Second Language to adults at a learning center approximately thirty miles east of Manhattan. Classes are free and there's usually a waiting list to get in. Due to the high demand, there's pressure on me not to fall short. I'd like to be remembered as something more than just a conjugator of verbs. I want to do right by them.

So I make sure the accent isn't too thick, thinning it out, slowing it down until I become the friendly anchorman in their living rooms. I finally learn the difference between lay and lie and who and whom, grammatical conundrums that have plagued me for years.

The students often tell me how American I look, but my looks are just a product of an earlier postcard. One day the faces they see in their living rooms will look like them.

Sometimes they forget my name and simply call me what I am.

"Tee-chur? What this mean? How you say?"

They regard my profession with the same esteem we hold for the family minister or doctor. It's difficult to receive at first, the complete opposite of the *My-Taxes-Pay-Your-Salary!* attitude from other teaching experiences.

Some of the men have dirt beneath their nails and smudges on their clothing from working long hours in fields and restaurants, while women chat about raising other people's kids. This is the first wave, the foundation builders for future generations. Railroads were built on the same principle, as well as buildings, bridges, and armies.

I welcome every new arrival with the same question:

"Where will you be staying?"

"With my aunt."

"My cousin."

"My father."

"My brother."

This is how it's always been done.

Each night we try to get something down on paper, an opinion on a current event, but tonight there is only one event. Nowhere else exists but there, about an hour's drive from here. Newscasters have started calling it Ground Zero. I commend everyone for coming to class on such a day. My students are quiet and still, a reverence I can best describe as noble. I am the only one in the room that was born here.

Weeks later, Ali confesses that his children tease him about his accent. Do I happen to have any accent ridding books? I tell him to just keep coming to class. We'll work on our accents together. When he reads his written work, it depicts his eldest son escaping from the sixty-seventh floor of a tower right after the second explosion. Ali is one of them men who prays before class.

When break is over, I interrupt the easy Spanish that many of them use. Class resumes and I start to pace the aisles, fragrances from the ladies' perfumes sweetening the air like their voices. A child sits in a corner doing homework, no trace of her mother's accent when she speaks. We begin our lesson.

"Okay, ready? I'm *laying* the pen down, but now it *lies* there on its own. See? *Lay. Lie.*"

They nod and take notes.

At the end of each semester we take a group picture. Everyone smiles and says, 'cheese!' I place each photo on the wall beside the first until it forms a narrative, a storyboard to some great experiment that's just getting started.

J. Bryan McGeever

Straight to Hell: A Teacher's Odyssey of Disgrace[xx]

It's official. I just drooled on myself while taking a nap in the NYC Department of Education's infamous *Rubber Room*. I was one of them now, and there was no turning back. After countless hours of reading or staring out the window watching jets takeoff from LaGuardia, my eyelids started to droop and there I was, wiping spittle from my chin before anyone noticed. But no one ever did, for inside these rooms everyone was immersed in their own story. You see, the first rule of the Rubber Room was that no one ever stopped talking about why they were sent to the goddamned Rubber Room. There was so much hurt, frustration, and downright paranoia inside this building, so many conspiracy theories, real and imagined, that the only way to get through another day was to let my head slip to my chest and dream about catching one of those jets to someplace else.

Even though the NYC Department of Education and the United Federation of Teachers recently agreed to end the practice of sending teachers to reassignment centers while awaiting disciplinary hearings, in late May it was my turn to take the walk of shame. I'd been assigned to the 4th floor of an office building pending investigation, yet every teacher in the city called it the *Rubber Room*, a theatre of the absurd starring pedagogues accused of assorted wrongdoings. Except for some houseplants and carefully marked calendars, the place was completely bare.

I gingerly stepped behind a glass partition to be greeted by a chorus of jailhouse terms like, "Fresh fish!" and "New meat!"

If you must know, I never saw the kid coming. He was an IEP student who was supposed to have been accompanied by a Special Education teacher. She was out that day. As I was conferring with a student after the bell, the boy took a running start from the hallway, really just to amuse himself, and hit me on my blind spot. The two of us crashed hard against the whiteboard and my instincts took over. I shook him several times by the shirt, asked him what the "fuck" he thought he was doing, and then let him go. I'll never forget the ripple of astonishment that overtook his face, his eyes widening in disbelief. He was simply unable to comprehend the consequences to his actions. I had no intent to harm him. My brain signaled an attack, so I reacted. When I produced the police report I'd filed for assault and emergency room x-rays to the DOE investigator, the man simply grinned and confirmed all charges. I didn't know this yet, but I'd eventually be fined eight thousand dollars for verbal abuse and corporal punishment.

Back at the rubber room, the lifers insisted upon an informal orientation. I was issued a seat then got to know the gang whether I cared to or not. There were saddened loners and feverish ramblers, wizened prophets, and total bullshit artists. I spotted two colleagues from my former building with six years on the floor between them. They smiled back like a pair of ghosts. Someone asked if I'd like to join their afternoon Scrabble tournament, and it struck me for the first time that my individual story, like all the others in this room, had been put on ice.

My cell phone rang, and a tired voice identified itself as the borough chapter leader. "Do not speak to anyone about your case…and be patient," was the summation of his advice. But because the DOE handled each case at such a glacial pace, telling one's tale became the major pastime. There were long winded speeches and frustrated monologues about injustice, a backlog of stories aching to be freed, just one long moan of complaint day after day.

A man eventually identifies himself as the floor's unofficial chapter leader and tells me what to expect. "Within a few weeks," he begins, "you'll receive your official charges via certified mail. Any wrongdoing committed by a student or administrator will be eradicated from the report so that it appears on paper as if you decided to go insane."

"In time, you'll be called to the Office of Special Investigations to discuss these allegations. They'll allow you ample time to complain and then confirm all charges..." Every word this man said turned out to be true.

As the days dragged through June, tension reached a fevered pitch. It was just a matter a time before the first warning shot was fired. It was usually a battle over turf, a room, a chair, the placement of a desk. They threatened to tell security, to write each other up, to call the police over perceived threats and insults. It was really no one's fault, for none of us should have ever met. No matter what the charge, guilty or innocent, we were simply being dehumanized. I tried to communicate this once to a pair of teachers pushing a desk into one another, but they weren't having it. The total annihilation of the other was the only thing that mattered.

Outside the window of the reassignment center that I now called home, another jet from LaGuardia shimmered in the sun. It gained momentum over Citi Field then cruised by our window and out of sight. Whenever I slept inside the Rubber Room, in my dreams I was never a disgraced teacher, and I awoke with the knowledge that this particular story would not define me.

J. Bryan McGeever

Theatre Thugs^{xxi}

As an obsessive theatregoer, I've always taken my responsibility as an audience member quite seriously. The phone ringers and candy eaters, the chronic sneezers and hacking coughers, those who laugh at nothing, and the ones who leap to their feet for no apparent reason, all irk me. For years, I believed they were *The Others*: philistines sent to jeopardize the sanctity of the boards. I was the patron who understood his role, sitting ramrod straight and attentive in my seat, chin slightly upturned. Should a prop fall into my lap—a piece of cork, a scrap of paper—I treated it like an artifact from another dimension, a place of wonder that I adored. I even adopted Frederick Exley's credo from *A Fan's Notes*: "I understood…that it was my destiny to sit in the stands with most men and acclaim others. It was my fate, my destiny, my end, to be a fan."

But then, like a clueless actor saying "*Macbeth*" backstage, I fell victim to a curse. Inside a darkened theatre one evening, a cell phone began to chirp. I glanced around for the offender and shook my head. *People…they're the worst.* Through a fog of righteous indignation, I eventually processed the brightly lit screen beside me, my fiancée, Tiffany, fumbling for the off button. The spine-tingling shame that followed has never quite left me.

The actor onstage broke character immediately. "Will-you-shut-that-thing-off!? Thank you!" He seemed close enough to touch, this thespian pausing in the middle of actual tears to administer swift justice before returning to the land of make-believe. I don't recall much after that. I may have suffered a bout of hysterical blindness, although I do remember our swift exit from the theatre, a small, dank basement on a quiet street in the Village. There was a curtain of some sort, a polite round of applause, and then a quick getaway up a narrow flight of stairs. The climactic escape from *The Shawshank Redemption* came to mind. We hit the welcome gloom of a hot, cobblestone street and seethed at one another.

"I can't believe you did that!"

"It wasn't me! It turned itself on."

"Who was on the phone, your mother? It's always your mother."

"Hey, watch it. Anyway, he should never break character. Yale Drama, sure, bud. You should have tossed him into the audience."

"You should have had your phone off!"

"I told you, it turned itself on!"

"Tiff, we're teachers- in New York City. We tell kids to put phones away for a living."

And so it went. It was her. It was me. It was Colonel Mustard with the candlestick in the library. I'd call out every infraction, minor to her, major to me. Eventually, our friends started calling us Mr. and Mrs. Booth, as in John Wilkes. We were *those* people now, a pair of theatre thugs, and I was inconsolable.

Then one night I had a revelation. We were attending another performance in orchestra seats, my beloved there beside me in a deep, peaceful slumber, her small frame sinking lower and lower into her overpriced chair. I nudged her awake. "Shakespeare? Really? I thought you loved teaching this play."

She craned her neck, realizing where she was. "I do, sweetie, but Caitlyn Jenner's no Lady Macbeth."

"That-is-not Caitlyn Jenner!"

As we headed home beneath the stars and the moon and the lovely breeze rolling off the Hudson, it hit me. Relationships are all about compromise. Perhaps it was high time to accept our fate as the Lucy and Ricky of NYC theatre going.

When we reached the subway, I called out to her. "Hey."

"What?"

"I hear Patti LuPone's playing Lincoln Center this summer."

"So?"

I pointed to the phone in her hand. "Why don't we give her a ring during act one?"

Maybe our daughter will inherit the theatre-addict gene from her old man. One can only hope.

J. Bryan McGeever

Book Review: *Intern Nation: How to earn nothing and learn little in the brave new economy* by Ross Perlin[xxii]

Every *Seinfeld* fan recalls the episode where Jerry's wacky neighbor incorporates himself and takes on a young intern named Darren. Darren's duties at *Kramerica* included laundry detail and scheduling high tea with a certain Mr. Newman. We laughed because it was clever. It didn't matter that the kid was being used, that he was wasting money on empty credits and ridiculous experiences. Sanity prevailed in a neat twenty-two minutes when his college dean put a stop to it. But what if no one comes to Darren's aid? What if he's not really a bit player on a sitcom, but a symbol of something real that's taking place globally right now? The joke is no longer funny, and the laugh track that follows each one of Cosmo's draconian demands becomes grotesque and more than a bit shameful, which is precisely why Ross Perlin includes the dialogue from this episode in an opening chapter of *Intern Nation: How to Earn Nothing and Learn Little in the Brave New Economy (Verso, $22.95)*.

Perlin, a native of New York City and graduate of Stanford, explores the essence of what it means to

103

be an intern in this impressive muckraking expose. Who are these people and what exactly do they do? Interns might fetch coffee or do cartwheels in a Mickey costume. Some write speeches for senators, while others make copies like nobody's business. Sometimes they're paid a minimum wage, sometimes not. They're the privileged children of country club buddies from New Haven, but also that scholarship kid who crashes on friends' couches while he works for free. The intern could be just about anybody and do just about anything, which is why their waters are often so muddied. "The very significance of the word *intern* lies in its ambiguity," Perlin explains.

The author begins his quest by describing a recent visit to Disney World: "The curtain rises…interns are everywhere…Even Mickey, Donald, Pluto and the gang may well be interns…" Disney has playfully confounded us with its brand of hocus pocus for generations, yet that's nothing compared to the way it's completely re-imagined the role of the college intern.

In exchange for the prestige of the Disney name on a resume, interns 'earn their ears' by working completely at the company's will. "Disney has figured out how to rebrand ordinary jobs in the internship mold," Perlin begins, "framing them as part of a structured program…without sick days or time off, without grievance procedures, without guarantee of workers' compensation, or protection against harassment or unfair treatment." Despite these harsh working conditions, between 7,000 and 8,000 college students arrive each year to Disney to do the Mouse's bidding. "'We're there to create magic,'" one intern told the *Associated Press.*

As Super Bowl winning quarterbacks continue to flock to Disney World, the same can be said for Chinese nationals. Once Disney's HR team realized the big savings it was enjoying by having a perpetual workforce of temporary employees, they decided to go a step further. Based on the J-1 Exchange Visitor Program, Disney's international internship program was born. "Workers brought in from hundreds or thousands of miles away are always easier to control, even more so if the legality of their presence depends entirely on the employer."

At least Disney goes through the machinations of a genuine internship for college credit. At The University of Dreams, a ten-year-old company located in Redwood City, California, there are no real students taking notes simply because there are no professors handing out assignments or grades. "That's right, you pay 'U of D' $1,000 per week to work, which makes college tuition look cheap." Perlin reveals how the company makes no effort to ensure its clients of a paid internship, which brings up the question of who should actually be paid for their work.

Unless an internship offers a substantial training program, and many do not, then an intern is considered an employee entitled to minimum wage and other protections under the Fair Labor standards Act (FLSA). The author wonders why no one's blowing any whistles, and the answer is quite sobering. The employer/intern relationship hinges on power: contacts, references, and impressive looking resumes. Should interns start shaking up the workplace, demanding fair pay and treatment, it would completely defeat their purpose. How will they ever make it onto the 'A' team if they don't prove themselves to be team players? The economic impact of all this free labor by willing victims is jaw dropping. "Using up to date, but still conservative figures (500,000 unpaid interns at the 2010 federal minimum wage), the money that organizations save through internships approaches $2 billion annually."

Despite this lack of compensation, a recent national survey revealed that one out of eighteen college freshmen expected to become an actor, musician, or artist. "This is where 'the rock-star jobs' and the glamour internships are—the more glamour perceived, the more vital connections, and the less likely it is that pay will ever enter the question." The dreams and desires of young people are as strong as ever, but without financial backing of some kind, how long can they actually pursue these interests? "Perhaps more than ever before, the rich are working and dominating particular industries." Perlin interviews a young art history major named 'John' about his interning experience at an auction house to illustrate the point. "'...One of the interns I was working with was literally royalty. The amount of work she was ready to do was next to nothing. Her father is a customer.'"

This disturbing trend continues in Washington where, "job creation is preached, not practiced." One Capitol Hill intern informs Perlin that out of every thirty interns, twenty-five of them may be 'packed', an insider term for the children of donors, friends, and important constituents. No one is paid at either the Hill or White House, where even Obama characterizes the experience as 'answering the call to service.' Despite the famous scandals between politicos and interns that have rocked the nation, the author maintains that this shameful practice is very much alive and well. According to veteran political analyst Andrew Sullivan, some Washingtonians simply refer to their interns as 'the flesh'.

Perlin's timely book raises many questions about the future of our country. Critics might describe it as one sided or accuse the author of axe grinding if it weren't for the fact that the book is so well written and thoroughly researched. Its message leaves us slightly stunned and more than a bit illuminated. Are interns taking their future into their hands, paying their dues until they've earned their way into a chosen field, or are they privileged children being handed something for nothing? The answer is both. Yet what does it say about a country whose art, music, film, and politics are fueled almost entirely by the wealthy? Why do the powerful prefer to exploit our young for little to no pay and give handouts to friends of friends rather than mentor our best and brightest?

Perlin offer solutions, yet even these hinge on powerful entities finally doing what's right. Colleges and universities must look out for their charges, keeping a safe distance from the "Wild West of sketchy internships," and the Department of Labor must enforce the law. The world at large needs to understand that the word 'intern' is actually a type of worker and not a student. Otherwise, Perlin suggests, it might be time to act. "A general strike of all interns would show all they contribute for the first time a delicious low-level chaos to the world's work." A low-level chaos, as I complete this review during the month of October in New York City, why does that phrase sound so eerily familiar?

J. Bryan McGeever

Diary Entry #1^{xxiii}

Dear Diary,

I'm pretty sure the doorman hates his job, manning the lobby of my Brooklyn apartment with the granite stare of a gargoyle. He looks more like someone waiting for a bus to get to work than someone who's already there. He's also enormous, slabs of muscle straining against his uniform as he scrolls through text messages for hours.

I actually prefer to open my own doors, but the guy comes with the building, his indifference at times reaching the level of performance art. I've even enlisted my three-year-old to try and break him, "Hey, Big Man!" she shouts, zipping past him on her scooter, but nothing.

Last year he handed me a package of gym equipment, shocking me as his lips began to move. He said he'd once tried out for the World Wrestling Federation, making it through several rounds before getting cut. I couldn't help but wonder what kind of persona he'd dreamed up for himself, something that lurked in shadow, dazzling the crowd with his astonishing powers of silence. He said it was the best time of his life. The next day he stared right through me, no doubt preparing for his comeback.

Diary Entry #2^{xxiv}

Dear Diary:

In 2002, I was completing my Master of Fine Arts degree at a local college. The writing program held a fund-raiser at the Culture Project on Delancey Street. The evening was hosted by George Plimpton and featured a panel of luminaries reading from their work.

My professor wanted two students to read as well, and I was one of those chosen. Among the impressive lineup that night was a Pulitzer Prize winner, a poet laureate, and some dude from Long Island trying not to hyperventilate.

I remember being distracted at the bright wall of light separating the stage from the audience and the awkward sound of my voice coming from the microphone. I finished my selection to polite applause and immediately began to question everything: *Had I picked the right story? Did I read it too fast? Does this haircut look stupid?*

As I returned to my seat, an elegant woman to my left smiled sweetly and reached out to me. I didn't know if she was congratulating me or if she just she felt sorry for a young man in over his head. All I knew was that Nora Ephron had just patted my knee.

The Paper Chase

I chase stories. The same way a memoirist returns to an integral part of his past or an ace reporter hunts down a lead, but different. I've been writing professionally for twenty-five years now. I've reported on school board meetings for the local town crier and written essays for the *Newspaper of Record.* My first job earned me forty bucks, my highest was two thousand. I keep copies of both checks in a scrap book.

As I settle into middle-age, all my youthful delusions have fallen away. I'm a journeyman. My writing routine is workman-like and blue collar, a player who's taken a few cuts in the majors, spending most of his career toiling in the minor leagues. I like to believe there's some dignity in refusing to quit.

Sometimes I place a flurry of three or four pieces at a once, newspapers, journals, magazines. Other times the publishing world reacts like I'm contagious. I used to keep rejection slips in a glass case to stay hungry. Now I submit by pressing a button, my sentences shooting into cyberspace to either find a home or drift off into oblivion.

Somehow, I've managed to jump out of the slush pile for over a quarter century. Yet each acceptance is so hard won that, when it finally makes its debut, I'm compelled to go out into the world and find it. It's mine after all, no matter what it says on the cover of any publication. I need to actually see it on paper to prove to myself that it's real. I've traveled down country roads in the Hamptons, subscribed to magazines I didn't want, and stumbled upon bookstores as small as walk-in closets just to feel the pages in my hands.

And I was doing it again, tracking down my latest essay, this time it was the Q train before sunrise, riding the rails through Brooklyn until I came upon a stack of newspapers on some dark, wet corner of New York. I just didn't know which corner. I got off at Atlantic to check the Barkley's Center, but all I found was its competitor smirking back at me. I tried Seventh Avenue and then DeKalb, but the news boxes were either empty or contained yesterday's news. I had one hour to get to work. My only option was to cross the Manhattan Bridge to the most famous slab of rock on earth. I got off at Canal and headed up Broadway, a street synonymous with success, but all its lights seemed to be out.

I headed deeper into Broadway, checking my watch, growing frustrated as I tried to beat the sun. By the time I came upon the publication, I clutched it like a found child. I knew the story of its life, from inception to print, from a fistful of post-it notes to the editorial section of this paper, and we were reunited. I grabbed five copies and hopped into a cab.

I once had a professor who was travelling her own journey. Her father had been a giant who'd written the consummate novel on The Great War. In order to feel her arrival as a writer, she believed it was necessary to spy some random stranger reading her work, an interesting challenge for her, but highly unlikely for me. I got back on the train and sat next to a woman who was indeed reading the same newspaper I'd just hunted down. I glimpsed my by-line over her shoulder, my sullen face staring back at me. She left the paper behind when her stop came up. So I snatched that one up, too.

One Last Thing Before I Go^{xxv}

Long Island's North Shore is solid and doesn't give way until spring. But there have been times, after hours of toil, where I've stood thigh deep in one of its holes and knew I'd accomplished something. It takes skill and determination to dig in this ground.

There's no finer way to honor home than to eat its food. "These are Long Island potatoes," my mother would say as we sat down to dinner. "This corn was picked yesterday." There was an implicit understanding that food grown on Long Island was special because it came from the same place we did.

Another way to respect home is to place something inside it for safekeeping, a time capsule or beloved friend. I've buried many dogs in Long Island's unrelenting soil. Each one had lived a good life here and this is where they belonged.

There's a plastic urn that I keep in my home in Brooklyn. Every time I move, I invariably find a spot for it on a shelf, a closet, or windowsill. It's supposed to contain the remains of my childhood dog, Major. Instead of returning him to the ground where he belonged, I tried to keep him forever. Now all I've got is this urn.

Years ago, my family paid a substantial sum to a place called *The Long Island Pet Cemetery*. The business turned out to be a sham. Plots were discovered unkempt and mass cremations were performed on animals whose owners had requested individual remains. If you'd paid for *Scruffy's* ashes, there was a good chance you received pieces of *Snowball, Annie,* and *Skipper,* as well. Animals too big for the furnace were just tossed into a ditch in the woods. Major was enormous, a Great Dane/Newfoundland mix. I know these people tossed my dog into a hole and left him there, the kindest soul I've ever known.

This urn I've been carrying around for years contains nothing more than scraps of other people's pets. I'm well aware that this is a First World problem, but a body riddled with cancer that keeps getting up to be at its master's side is heroic, be it animal or man. A spirit so strong it must eventually be put down by a veterinarian's needle deserves to be mourned.

The cemetery was shut down, its owners fleeing to various parts of the country to escape lawsuits, jail, and death threats. A memorial was held that summer, a candlelight vigil for dear friends. A member of the Jackson family even showed up to lend her support, not one of the original five, but still. The whole thing was very American.

There's a portion of Steinbeck's *Of Mice and Men* that gets me every time, some dialogue that resonates whenever I teach it to a roomful of ninth graders. "I ought to of shot that dog myself, George. Shouldn't of let no stranger shoot my dog." Seventeen years later I'm still trying to connect this experience to something larger. My life's in Brooklyn now, but there's one last thing before I go.

The Melville Memorial Park in Setauket is beautiful in spring and filled with renewal. Wedding parties pose along its small stone bridge on weekends, while families cruise the oak lined perimeter, pointing out turtles and swans. My mom would bring me here for picnics as a kid. There's an arboretum behind the pond that's filled with bamboo, enough to wander through for hours.

The urn's dubious contents rattle in my hands as I approach the bridge. As bogus as this container turned out to be, it still feels like sacrilege to pry it open with a pocketknife, to shake it clean and watch the dust settle into the stagnant waters below the bridge, muttering the same sentence again and again until it feels just right, *Good boy, Major, good boy...*

Dear NYC *xxvi*

Do you see the lovely, little girl rushing up the steps of P.S.139 in Brooklyn? Yes, that's her, the one with the long, spiral curls. It's her first day of Pre-K, and she's mine.

As a teacher myself in the New York City Department of Education for fifteen years, I wanted to publicly announce that I've been nothing but kind, generous, and compassionate to every kid who's ever stepped inside my classroom. The boy who received a perfect score on his Regents exam, as well as the one who threatened to set my hair on fire. The young lady who read her poem in Urdu at the city-wide competition and brought the house down, as well as the boy who said he'd shoot me after school. The student from Guinea who handed me a note regarding her genital mutilation as a child, and the boy who came out to me in a personal essay. The one who blindsided me into a blackboard, and the one who waited tables at the local IHOP. The nineteen-year-old who laughed when I caught him having sex with a fifteen-year-old girl in a stairway, and every kid who's called me a punk-ass-bitch before eight-thirty in the morning for the past fifteen years.

There has never been a single child in New York City, in or out of my classroom that I've treated with malice or not offered compassion and forgiveness. You have my word on this.

And now it's time to return the favor.

For forty-something years I've dreamed awfully big dreams. Every single one has turned to dust except for the vision walking up those stairs. You will cherish and honor every second that she graces your hallways. I've seen this system at its worst and you will not be sneaking anything past me, understood?

Some of the most shocking, eye-popping experiences I've had in my adult life have taken place inside NYC public schools, and I'm not talking about troubled kids. I witnessed Bloomberg era cruelty first hand. I saw what you did to those teachers. I watched you starve those kids of funds so you could gain control of their buildings, and I'm keeping a watchful eye on the current administration's handle of mayoral control, as well.

The largest school system in the country still has no true path as to where it is headed. Although, there is one certainty. Every day that I entrust you with my daughter's care, she will come home safe and happy and excited about the world, otherwise, you'll have a lion at your door roaring very specific questions.

Frankly, New York, I don't particularly trust you. I think you're mostly hype with a wicked mean streak. The 'danger and romance' you offered in my

twenties and thirties no longer appeals to me.
Broadway, Central Park, and the Brooklyn Bridge
still leave me in awe but lose their luster once I admit
that your school system has left me frazzled and
shell-shocked. Its instability, indifference and lack of
true leadership, I swear most times it appears you're
making it up as you go along. I just received word
that my school district has changed yet again. At this
point, I no longer bother asking why. It's just your
way.

So, I've got my supplies ready for another year,
and I'll get that bulletin board decorated tomorrow
because we both know that I'm decorating it just for
you. It presents a good front, doesn't it? But there's
one thing different about tomorrow. It's the first
time you'll be seeing me as a parent, which brings us
back to the little girl on the steps. Unfortunately,
New York City Department of Ed, you're all we've
got right now. So this is just a note from a father
wishing you a very successful school year.

Eulogy for James

Good afternoon and thank you for coming today. St. Ignatius has always been an important part of my extended family's history. I'm grateful that my Dad's service could take place here today. He went to grade school here. He was an altar boy for masses said in Latin. He married my mom here. I'm going to talk a bit about my dad, as well as the large, significant family in which we both belong.

For some time now, our particular branch of the family has resided in Brooklyn, and Brooklyn truly has it wonders, layers of important American history, but my family and I are not Brooklyn people. We're Long Islanders, and we hail from a large and wonderful clan of Irish-Italian Long Islanders. Before I go any further, there are times when I've taken this clan for granted, not appreciated it properly. But my mother and I cherish every one of you and love you unconditionally. It's taken me perhaps a half-a-century to realize that all of us are a part of something powerful and unique.

In order for any sizeable clan like ours to survive it must widen and shift, expand and replenish itself. Over periods of time, its top layer will be peeled back and those inside, our elders, must move on, and they will move on whether we like or not. Yet if we truly believe in our people, in our upbringing, then this is just a test of faith. Every time one of us passes, we bow our heads and mourn, we hold onto each other, and we carry on. This is our way, and it's the only way.

Lately, since the turn of the century, our top layer has been pried open repeatedly, our family's patriarchs leaving us one by one: my grandfather James, George, Joseph, and John. Our matriarchs, Fran, Ann, and June, and dear Rose currently preparing to leave this world. The image of all these souls, including Chris and Jimmy, receiving my father in Heaven brings my mother great comfort and joy.

Unfortunately, it's not always the top layer that leaves. There are those who have left too soon, and now my father has joined their ranks. This was not the plan, we tell anyone who'll listen. There must be some kind of mistake. We simply can't understand because we're not meant to understand. If we do have faith, all of this will be revealed to us at a later date.

So yes, off the record, if you spoke to me last Wednesday, I would have told you that this was all a sick joke. No chance to say goodbye? Are you kidding me? This was not his time, I would have said. It should have happened at least a decade later. If you spoke to me last week, I would have told you that the man got robbed. We think we eventually run out of tears, but we never do. An angry, young man can yell and scream and punch holes in the walls, and his beloved father will still be gone. Fortunately, a man of nearly fifty years understands that this is how it goes. These are the terms we're granted, and they are non-negotiable. We have no say in these matters, and it's all an integral and vital part of the mystery and beauty of life.

There are some famous lines from a D.H. Lawrence poem: *I never saw a wild thing sorry for itself. A small bird will drop frozen from a bough without ever having felt sorry for itself.* This was my father, James McGeever. He had his share of complaints, of course, because he was entitled to it. Tiffany and I had a gorgeous baby girl, and, because of our careers, it was best to reside in Brooklyn. Just like that, my parents moved from Florida and became Brooklynites. He did whatever work needed to be done in order to stay, to make his wife happy, to be with his son, and to have my daughter know and love him. And never did he feel sorry for himself. Having him for a father makes me a better man. Each time I stumble, which will consistently, I'll call upon him as a point of light for the rest of my days.

So as we gather today in Hicksville, perhaps it's more of a Hicksville of the past that we remember and hold so dearly, which is fine, a time when the town wasn't so spread out, the roads not so wide, the traffic not as thick, and my teenaged dad would hang from the wooden railroad crossing when the train approached and a guard in a small both would chase him away. Or he'd put on boxing gloves and slug it out with his cousin, Georgie, to the amusement of their grandfather and his pals. But no matter how far they widen the roads, no matter how many strip malls they build, I can still stand on the steps of this church and look upon the Hicksville where so many of my family members were raised.

I think everyone here is aware that our family has a storied past within the midget race car community, and that my great-grandfather's racing team was a powerful juggernaut for decades. It didn't matter if he was your father, grandfather, or great-grandfather, you simply called him Daddy Mike. His lovely, saintly wife was Nanny. And like all their descendants, my father adored Nanny and Daddy Mike, and he would tell me stories about them my entire life. These stories are told again and again until they become legend. So I may have a few of the details incorrect, but I prefer to remember it how Dad told it.

He said that whenever they arrived at a destination for a new race, Nanny would disassemble the parts of the engine, carefully cleaning each one, while Daddy Mike slept. In the morning, he'd awake to reassemble the parts while she slept, and I'm sure they both could have done it blindfolded. When my Dad told me this story it struck me as the purest form of partnership and union that I'd ever heard, that essentially the engine of this car was a symbol of their collective heart, entwined around this tiny vehicle. I feel it's our family's great story, and I love that my father passed it on to me. I'll re-tell it one day to Aubrey when she's old enough to understand.

I need everyone here to know that my mother and father had the same kind of love that Nanny and Daddy Mike shared. I was witness to it. Occasionally, it was a bit of a Bonnie & Clyde routine that drove me nuts, but it was strong and powerful. They met just a stone's throw away from here in the eighth grade. That simply doesn't happen anymore.

In high school, mom would gaze out of her classroom window, watching my father race up and down the block in a car he somehow finagled from a local bus driver. At the end of the day, he'd be there to pick her up, and for the next fifty years or so, Jamie would always be there to pick Barbara up. My mother's lost the other half of her heart, and she is crushed, but the family will hold her, and she'll carry on, using her husband as a point of light for the rest of her life.

About a year ago, I had this fantastic dream. It's normally best to keep our dreams to ourselves, but I'll share this one. It was one of those rare, remarkably lucid dreams that spring from our

J. Bryan McGeever

subconscious or who knows where. The kind of dream we never want to leave. I came upon this small, empty house, a familiar one, but one I hadn't been inside since the mid-seventies. It was my great grandfather's house, and as I entered, I knew there would be a piano against the wall for Chris to play at Christmas. I travelled through the living-room, into the kitchen, eventually reaching the back door. Outside, however, it wasn't Nanny & Daddy Mike's regular backyard, but a magnificent strip of beach with a brilliant sun shining down, and everyone was there, the entire tribe of us, and the food, of course, was incredible, before the entire scene dissolved the way dreams always do.

Afterwards, I thought about it for a while. What was its purpose? Did it mean anything, or was it just a bunch of nonsense until I understood that, of course, paradise for our clan would be a gorgeous strip of beach in Daddy Mike's backyard. Of course, it would. So I have to believe that my Dad is on this beach right now. Even though my faith as a Catholic has waned, I have to believe that he's there with everyone else, the whole Fam-damily. And so James, all I have to offer today are these words, but I can assure you that one of these days, we will join you on that beach. Thank you.

A Sports Coat is Worth Two Thousand Words

My dad reached inside the closet for his new jacket, single breasted, two button, and straight off the rack. It was pencil gray with flecks of black in it and may have had those professorial looking patches on the sleeves, but I'm not sure. He didn't care much about clothes and the jacket was nothing special. "See this baby?" he said, holding it by its hanger. "This is the coat I'll be buried in." He gave it a quick onceover before putting it back. "A little tight in the chest though."

I told him not to worry. Once he was in the ground he was bound to drop a few pounds. "Pretty soon, it'll be hanging off your shoulders." We called it the *Death Diet* and had a good laugh. The man was only two decades older than me. He wasn't going anywhere. But still, he didn't enjoy turning seventy and was referencing his mortality way too often. "Your mom's ninety-four," I assured him. "You'll cruise straight through your eighties." He'd smile back and shake his head.

In my classroom I keep a calendar that my students use to track time, field trips, vacations, and birthdays, marking off the days until something special arrives. For the past three months I've been doing it, too, counting up while they counted down, penciling in a number at the top of every box. On January 2nd, I'd rushed from my classroom in Jamaica, Queens to Brookdale Hospital in Brownsville. When I returned two weeks later, the calendar and blackboard still read January 2nd, as if my classroom had frozen until I returned. As of right now, my father's been dead for ninety days.

There's no reason to mark time in a datebook when the final number is forever, but I do it anyway, a tiny stab of pain every time the pencil touches paper. My dad had suffered an unexpected, massive heart attack at work. I've heard people call this the widow-maker and that's exactly what it did. My mother's still devastated, and I've lost the one guy who'd been rooting for me since birth. Like many fathers and sons, sports had been an overriding factor to our relationship.

I've never had an aptitude for numbers. When forced to memorize a series of digits as a kid I'd use a mnemonic device, assigning an athlete's jersey number to the corresponding numeral. If a friend's phone number was 393-5142, I'd recall it as Csonka-Ruth-Butkus-Robinson. Each of these players had been introduced to me by my dad, countless hours of watching and playing sports until the athletes and their jerseys were ingrained as one. I still apply this method to license plates while sitting in traffic or remembering a street address. The morning I returned to class, I marked the second day of my father's passing and said, "Number two, Derek Jeter." The seventh day had to be Mickey Mantle. Twelve, of course, was Namath. Sixteen was my jersey number in high school. The numbers on the calendar piled up quickly, straight past the double billing of Reggie Jackson and John Riggins, reaching Al Toon and Mark Bavaro in no time at all. Until today at ninety, the unbreakable Dennis Byrd. I don't know what happens once I reach one hundred days. I suppose I'll find some other way to grieve.

My dad had looked good at his wake, his casket flanked by flowered wreaths. A tight band of matriarchs, aunts, cousins, and godmothers, had come forward to make sure that every detail was perfect. He was laid out in his new sports jacket, black tie, and the crisp, white oxford shirt I'd purchased at a nearby mall. The beard he'd worn since he left the military was neatly trimmed, a set of rosary beads draped across his hands. The man looked sharp.

There was one other detail that stood out, something that set off a wave of magical thinking that's often needed at times like these. Somehow the right side of my father's sealed lips had been curved into a smile, something one might find on a sly, cartoon fox or rascally rabbit, a guy who was pleased with things, a man who knew that everything would be alright. I watched loved ones approach his casket, gesture to his face, and smile back. There was no smile, of course, just some happy accident that brought us comfort or perhaps the latest fad in mortuary science. Maybe some hotshot embalmer was leaving wry grins as a trademark to show off his skills. It made my mother happy, though, so we'll call it a smile.

We'd always been affectionate with each other, but had never really touched. I don't recall ever kissing my dad or even seeing him cry. Those barriers fell away the moment he'd died. In the hospital I'd peppered his forehead with kisses, wiped some blood from his lips, and cried into his already pale face. I continued touching him throughout his wake, stroking his beard and rubbing his chest, while my daughter tugged at one of his earlobes. At four, she's got a thing for lobes and his were the best.

Conversation swirled about the room as I tended to the casket. Oddly enough, the surreal, cocktail party atmosphere of a traditional Catholic wake can be comforting. The place had a good buzz, family and friends catching up, making sure my mother was never alone. Amidst the scattered assemblies stood a large, older man with powerful looking shoulders and a stoic face I recalled from the eighties. We tend to forget how young these athletes are when they retire from their sport. This guy could've cleared the room with a raised eyebrow. I didn't know him, but he looked intelligent and kind, placid as he stood just a few feet away.

No one in my immediate family had ever met Marty Lyons, former New York Jets great and noted humanitarian. He was a friend of my aunt's family and was here to pay his respects to them. Lyons was a key member of the New York Jets Sack Exchange, along with Abdul Salaam, Mark Gastineau, and Joe Klecko, a defensive line so fierce it caused the NFL to start counting quarterback sacks as a statistic. As I stole glances his way, I realized he was the only member I'd never met. My dad had taken me to see Salaam at a local sporting goods store, and Gastineau, the colorful inventor of the "Sack Dance," had made an appearance at my football camp in feathered hair and gold chains, bare-chested and glistening. I met Klecko years later, where a few good natured Gastineau jokes delighted the audience, but I'd never met Lyons. His presence at the wake flooded me again with boyhood memories of sports and my father.

An eighties childhood on Long Island was idyllic, although somewhat limiting for kids not yet old enough to drive. I'd often come home from team practice just to play more sports until dark, the sonic pop of aluminum bats hitting tennis balls, the shadowy outlines of footballs jamming fingers and smacking faces at sundown. My dad would hit pop flies or play official quarterback whenever called upon.

If my friends and I ran out of actual sports to play we'd just make one up. We kept hearing about some idiocy called fireball, a demented version of dodgeball where every player was already a loser, and were compelled to try it. Simply dip some tennis balls in gas, light them on fire, and let the fun begin. During the hysteria of swatting and kicking explosives at my best pals, a ball stuck to the top of my right sneaker, singeing quickly through its mesh and leaving a gaping hole. I got so panicked I ended up burying it in the backyard without a second pair for backup. The next day at Little League, all eyes were on the kid digging into the mound in a pair of brown loafers.

My father arrived from work to see his son pitching in church shoes. When irritated, the Long Island accent would get thicker. "Bryan," he said as I tried to reach the dugout, "what-da-hell-iz-is? Where's da sneakas we jus' ga-choo?"

"Dad, I have no idea…"

It's easy as an adult to look back and romanticize the bond my father and I shared through sports, although we did have our share of *Great Santini* moments. Times when his interest in my athletic career greatly outweighed my own. As my body started to change, the baby-fat seemingly melting away overnight, I was no longer the husky lineman on the football team, but a running back who worried if he was fast enough to play the position. The instant I scored my first touchdown, a sixty yard, out-of-body experience that's still the closest I've ever come to achieving pure bliss, I became fascinated with speed. When baseball season arrived that year, I went out for track instead.

My father invariably believed that being a natural left-handed pitcher would be my "ticket" to great things. We couldn't have a simple catch on the front lawn without it turning into some kind of training session. The day I told him I was no longer a baseball player, the ball sailed way over my head and I was instructed to go get it. I rummaged through some bushes forty yards away, trotted back, and handed him the ball. He held it up between us. "You ready to throw now?"

"Nope."

He chucked it again, the ball skipping halfway down the block this time. "Then take a walk, pal. We can do this all day." He wasn't taking my retirement very well, although one of the last things we did before my parents moved was have a catch on that same front lawn, our arms aching from throwing muscles not used in decades.

I was never anything special on any diamond, track, or football field. Like so many other kids, I had my moments, my dreams quickly surpassing my ability. It's clear to me now that the most important aspect of any competition is the people who show up to watch us compete. I could stand on any athletic field in the county, look over a shoulder, and there he'd be, a smile, a nod, or thumbs up for every punt, pass, or kick. I teach in New York City at a mostly fatherless high school. Many of the problems that haunt these teenaged boys could be soothed by one good man watching them from the stands.

I'd once carelessly given my dad directions to the wrong high school- Smithtown East not West. By the time he arrived to the game it was over. As I began to describe the pass I'd caught for a touchdown, this high, arcing spiral that still inhabits my daydreams, his face dropped and he looked hurt. It was common knowledge in our family that it was *his* job to watch me score and I had broken our pact. My dad rooted for me to succeed up until the moment his heart stopped beating. I am the proverbial fortunate son.

※※※※※※

I eventually went over to Marty Lyons and introduced myself. We shook hands and I thanked him for coming. He left having no clue what an important family circle he'd helped me complete. All it took was one retired, defensive lineman to kick start a wave of emotions I hadn't considered in years. I was very pleased that he'd been here. Later, I smoothed the lapels of my father's suit and spoke to him for the last time. "You see that? A Jet was here.

Ninety-three from the Sack Exchange…" My dad smiled.

He continued to smile as the lid of his casket was closed and then transported to Calverton National Cemetery, where my mother was presented with the American flag. Then my father's body would be placed into the Long Island soil, wearing his new sports jacket forever.

J. Bryan McGeever

About the Author

McGeever's stories have appeared in The New
York Times, Newsday, The Christian Science
Monitor, Writer's Digest, and The Southampton
Review. He teaches English in NYC public schools
and lives with his family in Brooklyn.

Small Rooms and Others

J. Bryan McGeever

About the Press

Unsolicited Press is a small press in Portland, Oregon. The team produces award-winning poetry, fiction, and creative nonfiction.

Learn more at www.unsolicitedpress.com

137

Small Rooms and Others

Acknowledgments

[i] Originally published in the *Long Island Newsday* (abridged)

[ii] Originally published in *The Brooklyn Eagle*

[iii] Originally published in *The Christian Science Monitor* (abridged)

[iv] Originally published in the *New York Post*

[v] Originally Published in the *Newtown Literary Journal*

[vi] Originally published in *AM New York*

[vii] Originally published in *Mr. Beller's Neighborhood*

[viii] Originally published in *TDF Stages Magazine*

[ix] Originally published in *The New Engagement*

[x] Originally published in the *East Hampton Star*

[xi] Originally published in the *Long Island Press*

[xii] Originally published in the *New York Times*

[xiii] Originally published in the *East Hampton Star*

[xiv] Originally published in *City Limits Magazine* (Independent Press Award); *Lost and Found: Stories from New York* (anthology)

[xv] Originally published in *Newsday*

[xvi] Originally published in *City Limits Magazine* (Independent Press Award); *Lost and Found: Stories from New York* (anthology)

[xvii] Originally published in *Chelsea Station Magazine*

[xviii] Originally published in the *East Hampton Star*

[xix] Originally published in the *New York Times* (abridged); *Family Circle Magazine* (abridged); *The Steinbeck Project Commemorative Journal* (anthology)

[xx] Originally published in *The Rockaway Wave* (abridged)

[xxi] Originally published in *TDF Stages Magazine*

[xxii] Originally published in the *East Hampton Star*

[xxiii] Originally published in the *New York Times*

Small Rooms and Others

---

^{xxiv} Originally published in the *New York Times*
^{xxv} Originally published in *Newsday*
^{xxvi} Originally published in *The Indypendent*